Living the Truth

Alan Jones

Living the Truth

Living the Truth

Alan Jones

COWLEY PUBLICATIONS
Cambridge · Boston
Massachusetts

Published in the United States of America by Cowley Publications, a division of the Society of St. John the Evangelist. No portion of this book may be reproduced, stored in or introduced into a retrieval system, or transmitted, in any form or by any means—including photocopying—without the prior written permission of Cowley Publications, except in the case of brief quotations embedded in critical articles and reviews.

Library of Congress Cataloging-in-Publication Data:
Jones, Alan W., 1940–
   Living the truth / Alan Jones.
        p.   cm.
   Includes bibliographical references.
   ISBN: 1-56101-183-5
   1. Truthfulness and falsehood—Religious aspects—
   Christianity. I. Title.
BV4647.T7 J66 2000
241'.673—dc21   00-043190

Scripture quotations are from the *New Revised Standard Version of the Bible*, © 1989 by the Division of Christian Education of the National Council of the Churches of Christ in the USA. Used by permission. All rights reserved.

Editor: Cynthia Shattuck
Copyeditor and Designer: Vicki Black
Cover design: Vicki Black

Cover art: Detail from *Mont Sainte Victoire* (1902-1904) by Paul Cezanne

This book was printed on recycled, acid-free paper by Data Reproductions in the United States of America.

Cowley Publications
28 Temple Place • *Boston, Massachusetts 02111*
800-225-1534 • *www.cowley.org*

On a huge hill
Cragged and steep, Truth stands, and hee that will
Reach her, about must, and about must goe;
And what the hills suddennes resist, winne so.

—*John Donne*

FOR KOSTA AND COOPER
AND FOR NEW BEGINNINGS

∾

Contents

Acknowledgments

I would like to acknowledge my gratitude for those who provided time, space, and inspiration which allowed me to write:

> my wife, Cricket, for her energy, imagination, and love in creating the inner space to work;
>
> for the community of Grace Cathedral, San Francisco, for understanding that time to think and write is not wasted;
>
> for Sally Jordan and Nancy Hamon, who made available free and open spaces in which to slow down;
>
> for Cynthia Shattuck, whose firm editorial hand rescued the work from some of its more disastrous meanderings.

Thank you.

∽

Preface

This book is divided into four parts: truth as fact, fiction, relationship, and mystery. These four levels of truth require hard work. Sometimes we will fail or come only to a partial knowledge. I know that often I am spiritually lazy with regard to seeking the truth. Sometimes the challenge and possibility of changing my mind and behavior is too costly. The truth that makes me free is, for the most part, the truth I prefer not to hear. Sometimes I do not want to know the answer badly enough to go to all the trouble of finding out. In fact, I go to a lot of trouble *not* to find out. I do not like to take the time to find out things I need to know. The pace of life and the speed of change make it difficult to slow down. *Truth takes time to reveal itself.* This story is told that when Chou En Lai was asked, "What do you think of the French Revolution?" he replied, "It's too early to tell!"

What, then, is truth? A crossword puzzle? A morass of facts that need to be ordered? A mystery in which we all live?

All three. The pursuit of truth never ends.

~

part one

Truth as Fact

∽

Chapter 1

The Truth About John

"How many of you know what is important?" Up went all the hands. "Very good," said Stuart, cocking one leg across the other and shoving his hands in the pockets of his jacket. "Henry Rackmeyer, you tell us what is important."

"A shaft of sunlight at the end of a dark afternoon, a note in music, and the way the back of a baby's neck smells if its mother keeps it tidy," answered Henry. "Correct," said Stuart. "Those are the important things."

—E. B. WHITE, *STUART LITTLE*

How do you know what is important? It isn't always easy to tell. Bombarded with too much information too fast, we easily get confused. How do you sort out one truth from another and then fit them all together? It looks easy when it comes to simple facts, but what about the deeper truths? Let's start our exploration with the hardest of all questions—not with the 2 + 2 = 4 kind of truth, but

3

the truth about you and me. Facts are important but, as we shall see, there is more to truth-telling than the gathering of facts. For a start, how do the facts of the world fit together? And how do you find a story that is faithful to the facts?

My friend John and I have known each other from college days. At that time he was conventionally religious in a detached and amused kind of way; I think he kept a toe in the door mainly because of nostalgia. Both his parents were dead and he had been raised in a bland form of Christianity that he had come to think of as weak and in need of protection. "A religion for losers!" he used to say to get me riled up. There was nothing risky, challenging, or revelatory about his childhood religion, no vindictive nuns or cruel pastors in his background to put him off it for life. Religion was at best pointless but harmless, and at worst, irrational and dangerous. John would show up in church several times a year, and he supported his wife Susan's going to church because it was "good for the children." Besides, the kids could make up their minds, as he had done, when they were older. But John had a problem. He drank. When he drank a little he became maudlin. When he drank a lot he became nasty. Things got so bad a couple of years ago that there had to be an intervention. He is now in AA.

❧ Truth and Trust

An acquaintance of mine confronted me the other day with a request for "the absolute truth" about our mutual friend John. I groaned inwardly, wishing he had asked me something easy, like "What is the capital of Romania?" or "What's the average annual rainfall in Montana?" These kinds of questions are easy to handle, and if I don't know the answers there are ways of finding out. Also, there is only *one* answer to these factual kinds of questions. But my questioner wanted to know something much more important about our friend John. Was he an alcoholic? If he was, how was he dealing with it? Was he dealing with it at all? As it happens, the question was not unreasonable because it had to do with hiring John to do an important job. But my questioner did not really need to know the absolute truth (as if *that* could be known about anyone) about John. He really wanted to know if John could be trusted. My acquaintance needed someone he could count on. Truth, in this case, was not so much a matter of fact as one of trust.

I knew John had stopped drinking and was a regular at the local AA meeting. But I was floored for the moment by the word "absolute." I lost sight of the reason for the question and went off in my head, running after questions like, "Who was John really? What is the absolute truth about John?" I began to wonder about the absolute truth about me and the world. My day-dreaming took me far away from the realm of hard facts and into the darker place of interpretation and faith. I found myself wandering in two worlds: the world of facts and the world of interpretation; the world of truths and the world of trust. When I think of John and all that he has been through, I wonder about the mystery of being human and realize that, in many significant ways, I am a mystery to myself. One part of that mystery is that, deep down, I trusted John. Why? There were lots of reasons *not* to trust him. Drink, after all, had almost wrecked his marriage.

It was John's great capacity for friendship and loyalty that enabled me to trust him. With a strong circle of support led by his wife and two young children, he made a fresh start. He was also good at his job although I often teased him for being a bit of a control freak. The first thing that came to me when I was asked for the truth about John was that he is a splendid person, radiant with delight and possibility. That is why I trust him. But I still can't get the word "absolute" out of my mind. I know it can be a dangerous word, suggesting rigidity of mind and coldness of heart. But it also points to something important. So I don't want to give up the word "absolute" altogether because John longs to know, as do I, who we are deep down, who we are "in the end" — finally and absolutely.

Writing in *The Boston Globe*, novelist James Carroll once asked a question: "What if human beings are never in full possession of the truth, but must constantly seek it in new experience in a dialogue of respect and mutuality with others? Does this equal relativism?" Such questions drove John crazy because it suggested a reality totally beyond his control. He had to learn that being open to new possibilities did not necessarily mean that anything goes. John defended his "absolute truths" with a passion that exhausted him and all those around him. Conversation became almost impossible when he drank: he always wanted to be on top of things and to win every battle. More often than not he did win because he was clever with words, but you could see that his victories left him empty and puzzled. It was as if he asked himself, "If I am right, why do I feel so empty?" Instead of realizing that truth is the horizon toward which we are always journeying, John wanted to possess it then and there. He wanted everything cut-and-dried, fully defined. He could not stand moral ambiguity. The notion that life might be a journey of discovery frightened him. He hated surprises. No wonder he drank. John had not yet discovered a basic truth about life.

   ✳ *We are pilgrims of the truth—we haven't arrived.*

When John did hit bottom, he had to go through a painful process of discernment with the help of a supportive community. John is an intelligent man, inventive and imaginative, but his pictures of reality were so real to him that he forgot they were merely *pictures*. John became so attached to the picture-book version of the world he had made for himself that he soon came to resemble the picture he had created. It wasn't a very happy one. His view of himself and his world were dominated by images of success and acquisition, with competition the grid by which he judged what was true and what was not. And up to a certain point he did well; he was one of the winners.

Like most of us, John was awash in information about what he thought mattered, but the information was useless because the connection between information and human purpose had been cut. What was the point of having a lot of facts at your fingertips when they didn't fit together in some purposeful way? He was often "right," but so what? Being right wasn't enough. He thought that the acquisition of information would give him some control over his life. He was shocked to discover that when information appears indiscriminately, directed at no one in particular, in enormous volume and at high speeds, it easily becomes disconnected from vision, meaning, or purpose.[1] No wonder John often felt overwhelmed by information, and angry and frightened that he had no control over it after all. It wasn't just useless. It was toxic. It not only didn't tell him what he needed to know, it often distorted what he already *did* know. When the tie between information and human purpose is severed, what use are little bits of information?

John is a bright man and he could see what was happening to him and to his world even though he was powerless to do anything about it. He was clogged up by pointless "facts" with no place to go, no way of fitting them together into a whole. He was sick of information-overload, sick of being "right," and sick of himself.

John first had to learn that *we are pilgrims of the truth—we haven't arrived.* And then another principle emerged.

    ☙ *Information is insufficient. It has to serve a higher purpose than itself.*

And what is that higher purpose? To find out, John had to give up his desire for control and begin a journey through his fears and resentments. He was a person who found the contradictions of human experience maddening. People were passionate, greedy, naive, ugly, and violent, but at the same time capable of trust, heroism, and love. He discovered that, deep down, he neither liked nor trusted his fellow pilgrims very much.

    There is a model of psychoanalysis that describes what happened to John. Psychoanalysis is a conversation for which people pay because the story they are telling themselves about their lives has stopped, or become too painful, or is damaging and enslaving to themselves and others. When this happens we look for another way of narrating our lives. We go shopping for myths and stories, particularly those that give us a reason to blame something or someone for our pain. The story John was telling himself about himself (successful businessman, *bon vivant*, great husband, good father) suddenly stopped. To his horror he watched himself become mean and violent, and kept on drinking in the hope that the story in its best form might revive. He slipped into the inner violence of depression as a means of coping. Sometimes he exploded violently outwards against others. His story dried up.

    When I was asked the absolute truth about John, I thought of Arthur Miller writing about his wife Marilyn Monroe at the time she was filming *The Misfits*. Miller witnessed her deterioration as she slid into the howling loneliness of depression and paranoia, relying on barbiturates to make it through the day. One evening an anxious Miller, worried to death, watched over his drugged and sleeping wife. "I found myself straining to imagine miracles. What if she were to wake up and I were able to say,

'God loves you, darling,' and she were able to believe it! How I wish I still had my religion and she hers."[2]

What was the truth about Marilyn Monroe? The truth about all of us? "God loves you, darling!" comes closer to the absolute truth than any phrase I know. When he hit bottom John's circle of family and friends communicated this basic love to him, and, at the same time, taught him something about truth: truth without love is a lie.

So what is the truth about you? The rock-bottom truth? Can the truth be told? Can the whole truth be told? Should it? Is the truth about us a kind of secret that has to be discovered? What is the place of love and compassion in truth-telling?

We are ready for our third maxim. Remember the first two? *We are pilgrims of the truth—we haven't arrived. Information is insufficient. It has to serve a higher purpose than itself.* Now the third:

> ❧ *In this poor world, only love can be entrusted with the truth.... When you're out hunting secrets, make sure you're looking for the right one.*[3]

Only love can be entrusted with the truth, and the truth about you is a complex and multi-layered story. Who would you trust to tell it? When it comes to the story of my life, I want the deepest and best interpretation put on it by a sympathetic narrator. Why? It's not simply a matter of self-protection but a matter of conviction that, when it comes to the truth about another person, compassion is the interpretive key.

The hero in the movie *American Beauty* knows that his wife and daughter think of him as "this gigantic loser." And that is what John thought he saw in the eyes of his wife and kids whenever they looked at him. In the movie, the father confesses, "They're right. I've lost something. I don't know what it is, but I know I haven't always felt this sedated. But it's never too late to get it back." In John's life, his family and friends communicated to him just how much he mattered to them, just how much he was loved. It was their belief in him that enabled John to discover a deeper truth about himself. He wasn't a loser, a drunk, a nobody, after all. Life became an adventure. John became a pilgrim of the truth—a man in touch with his own mystery. He began to recover something he had lost.

꩜ *Trust Love with the Truth*

When the pursuit of Truth with a capital T became a spiritual adventure for John, he discovered that one of the consequences was the dislocation of the structures that had enslaved and seduced him. Dislocation prepared him for revelation and opened him up to new possibilities. He began telling himself a new story, one in which everything he did made a difference, as though all eternity depended on it. It isn't that John has become fanatical about his actions. He simply woke up to the truth that he had only one life to live, that it wasn't a rehearsal, that we are mistaken if we think that we can stand on the sidelines of our lives and be spectators. John experienced Truth with a capital T as a summons truly to live and to be present to his own life and times. It rescued him from the crippling fear of being helpless. Years ago, he told me how scared he was by the thought of being incapacitated, of being out of control. He once asked me to promise "to make them pull the plug" on him if he were to be terminally ill. We talked of the humiliation of not being in control of one's bodily functions. He wondered if the dying, humbled, and humiliated self would be his true "self."

I couldn't help thinking about John when I read of the death of the novelist Iris Murdoch. She suffered from Alzheimer's disease and in the end, lost control of everything. Who was the *true* Iris Murdoch? She was a fine novelist and elegant philosopher; at the end, she was fearful, smelly, and eccentric. She once said, long before

Alzheimer's struck, that we are called to lead the life of virtue, the life of kindness, because that is all there is. This wonderful woman with a fine mind suffered the many indignities of her disease—not only the loss of her vital ability to think clearly, to remember, to communicate. But according to her husband John Bayley, she also showed Christ-like qualities of tolerance, amusement, and good nature. Who was she in the end? What was the truth about Iris Murdoch? Could she be reduced to the smelly, fearful creature who collected rubbish? The truth is that she was and is loved and lovable. This cannot be *proved*. All I can do is accept the invitation to *see*, really see, the world and invite you to do the same. When we really see, the only appropriate response is gratitude.

Iris Murdoch once described a simple incident. She is looking out of her window "in an anxious and resentful state of mind, brooding perhaps on some damage to my prestige. Then suddenly I observe a hovering kestrel. In a moment everything is altered. There is nothing but kestrel. And when I return to thinking of the other matter it seems less important." In an act of self-forgetfulness another and larger truth emerges. We call that act of self-forgetful contemplation—the act of seeing what appears to be "the sheer, alien, pointless, independent existence of animals birds, stones, and trees." This self-forgetfulness isn't self-annihilation, but a form of *pleasure*. It has to do with love, Murdoch wrote, which is "the extremely difficult realization that something other than oneself is real."[4]

I think this is what happened to John. He woke up and saw the world differently. Or, better, something woke up in him: a sense of wonder and gratitude even in the middle of all the mess and muddle of being human. After the intervention of his family and friends, John came out of his sedated state, sat up, and took notice. He would be horrified at the language, but in terms of the tradition he had rejected, John had been "born again." He got himself back. Like Iris Murdoch, who when asked if she were coming closer to God replied, "I think God is coming closer to me," John experienced the strange truth of a presence within himself of someone Other than himself.

What impressed John most about the truth-telling of his friends and family was not so much their willingness to confront him with some hard truths as the *way* in which these truths were communicated to him. The method and manner his friends and family chose to use (strong intervention with clear and uncompromising love) spoke to him of love, of a deeper truth about himself that enabled him to face some harsh realities without despair. He understood that truth is just as much a matter of the *way* truths are communicated as the truths themselves. For the first time, it dawned on him that the way the great questions of life are *framed* is as important as the questions themselves.

On one level he was a drunk, a loser, and a nobody, but that wasn't *all* he was. There was a deeper truth and it took others who cared about him to show him the way to his truer self. John had to discover that there were levels of truth about him that he needed to explore. Finally, he came to the fourth and most important thing he had to learn.

Remember the first three: *We are pilgrims of the truth—we haven't arrived. Information is insufficient. It has to serve a higher purpose than itself. In this poor world, only love can be entrusted with the truth.* Now he began to accept the fourth truth:

   ა *He was deeper and lovelier than he knew.*

John longed for this good news about himself as a drowning man longs for a lungful of air.

When a student went to his teacher to ask for enlightenment, the story goes, the master took him by the hand and led him down to the river where he held his student's head under the water. The young man, frightened and surprised, struggled for air. Because his teacher was strong he was able to hold the student's head under the water with tremendous force. With a supreme effort born of fear and anger, the student, fighting for his life, burst out of the water, and sucked in lungfuls of air. Panting on the river bank, he stared stupefied at his teacher, who said to him, "Until you want the truth as strongly and passionately as you wanted that breath of air, don't come to me asking for enlightenment!" There are many circumstances that can bring us to the point of such gasping for the truth. John's alcoholism brought him to the brink of the abyss. For others it can be a death, a divorce, the news of a terminal illness, being fired or "downsized." Almost anything that happens to us can turn into a wake-up call.

John longed for integrity, honor, and honesty in his life. It is easy to be cynical about such high-sounding words but our longing for them is like the gasping for breath of the student whose master held his head under the water. They are signs of our longing for a self at home with itself: clear, undivided, and joyful. As St. Teresa of Avila pointed out centuries ago, some of us never get beyond the courtyard of the interior castle that she called her self or her soul. We fear to go inside ourselves because of the betrayals and contradictions we might find there. John spiraled into despair when he faced the truths of a betrayed self. Like him, we want to be at home with ourselves and in the universe.

The truth about John? About me? About you? I know of only one way to get to the truth about what really matters. It is only by staying awake, being present, that we come to know what really matters. The discipline of sitting humbly before what presents itself to us day by day; the humility to wait for the revelation behind the myriad facts that present themselves to us at lightning speed everyday. Isabel Allende wrote about what really mattered in telling the story of the dying of her daughter, Paula. "I finally understood what life is about; it's about losing everything. Losing the baby who becomes a child, losing the child who becomes an adult, like the trees lose their leaves. So every morning we must celebrate what we have."

The truth about John? What have we discovered? John first had to wake up and open himself to a deeper truth about who he was. Second, he had to become an apprentice, or, better, he had to become a midwife assisting at his own rebirth. He discovered that being human was like learning a craft. Finally, he had to accept that the world needed him to be himself. There was a work for him to do in the world after all and only he could do that particular work. He became a pilgrim of the truth, drawn and informed by mystery.

What truth do you discern in "a shaft of sunlight at the end of a dark afternoon, a note in music, and the way the back of a baby's neck smells if its mother keeps it tidy"? To know the answer, wake up from your sedated state! Become an apprentice and learn the craft of being human. Accept that the world needs you. And remember the four maxims:

    We are pilgrims of the truth—we haven't arrived.

    Information is insufficient. It has to serve a higher purpose than itself.

    In this poor world, only love can be entrusted with the truth.

    You are deeper and lovelier than you know.

Chapter 2

Respect for the Facts

Information is insufficient. It has to serve a higher purpose than itself.

The novelist Lloyd C. Douglas lived in a boarding house when he was a student. On the first floor lived a retired music teacher, infirm and unable to leave his apartment. Every morning they had a ritual: Douglas would come down the steps, open the old man's door, and ask, "Well, what's the good news?" The music teacher would pick up his tuning fork, tap it on the side of his wheelchair, and say, "That's middle C! It was middle C yesterday; it will be middle C tomorrow; it will be middle C a thousand years from now. The tenor upstairs sings flat, the piano across the hall is out of tune, but, my friend, that is middle C!"[1]

There is something deeply satisfying about middle C always being middle C, but a liking for facts is more than a good feeling. It has to do with respect for the world as it presents itself to us. Middle C acts as a fixed point, a place from which to start. Like John, we must begin by taking notice and by sitting humbly before what is *there*. Accuracy is important and data are to be respected. It is only after these basic rules of accuracy are followed that the deeper truths are revealed. If we begin with sloppy or inaccurate information, we will soon find ourselves caught in a web of deception.

The place where you would expect respect for accuracy and for facts is the world of academia, especially in the pure sciences. Yet even there we find inquisitions and witch hunts over rival *stories* about truth. Identifying and penalizing false and dangerous opinions is alive and well in our universities. For example, in 1990 a university student was informed against for calling Martin Luther King, Jr. a communist. He was summoned to a hearing and punished for making incorrect and hurtful remarks during a conversation late at night. The issue, of course, is not whether his statement about King was literally true, but the fact that he was punished for saying so.[2]

Science can never be anything more than a disconnected number of observations of phenomena. There has to be some inclusive principle added to the process for science to function as a discipline. My friend John discovered that an inclusive principle of truth combines not only the need for facts but also the need for *narration*. John had had enough feedback to know *what* had happened to him and *how* it happened. What he couldn't figure out was *why*. Did the mess he was in have any meaning? For that he needed a way of telling a story about himself that was not only faithful to the facts, but also a doorway into a hopeful future.

Concern for truth cannot be taken for granted today. In a report of a conversation over a mission statement for a college of arts and sciences, some members of the faculty believed that the statement should include the phrase "concern for truth." The dean warned that the word "truth" makes people nervous. Truth, after all, is relative, isn't it? Besides, whose truth were we talking about?

Some of the faculty believed that to disagree about the truth makes all truth relative. How many times have I heard someone say, "You have your truth and I have mine." I reply, "No, you have your *perception* of the truth and I have mine." But it is almost axiomatic in academic circles to look down on those who have a concern for truth and favor instead what has been called the "higher dismissiveness"—the tendency to dismiss people who struggle to pursue truth as naive at best, and dangerous at worst.[3] Yet there is something to this point of view in that those who *think* they know and own the truth can do great harm. We know that what is actually true and what is *accepted* as true are not always the same. But why come to the cynical conclusion that bias is everywhere and objectivity impossible? Why reduce knowledge to a social construct of class, race, and gender? Then truth becomes merely a matter of tribal solidarity, a set of assumptions that the people I happen to agree with accept. In other words, truth is what I or my clan want it to be. Sometimes this is the case, but not always. If we are committed to accuracy we will not only acknowledge hard facts, like middle C, but also notice how facts are assembled and used for a particular purpose, not always benign.

So in some respects the "higher dismissives" are on the right track but they have made half of the truth—facts are sometimes subject to interpretation—into the whole truth—therefore there are no facts, only interpretations.[4] These half-truths are important in that they remind us that obnoxious theories (like the superiority of the white race) backed by a few facts are often used in ways that oppress people. Yet you can see how easy it is to move from saying that truths are made up by the dominant class to claiming that the pursuit of truth itself is dangerous. I once complained to a fellow priest that in our conflicts he didn't play fair. Because he saw the world through the prism of class, he replied, "Playing fair is middle-class!" Then I knew where he stood and we haven't had a serious conversation since.

Too often we seem to be able to see the truth only through a distorting prism—the prism of self-interest, self-preservation, or victimhood. There are, of course, true victims, people who have suffered horrible things, but there are also those who have assumed the mantle of victim without really earning it. Then they cling fiercely to their victim status because it has become their only known mark of identity. It is an interpretive key unlocking life's mysteries and the prism through which all experience is refracted.

The problem with the culture of victimization is that it obscures the real victims. That is one of the reasons why it is important to go on searching for the truth even though it is often messy and difficult. The alternative to being committed to accuracy and finding a story faithful to the facts is to be in perpetual war with each other: my claim to truth is as good as yours, and if I happen to be bigger and stronger, so much the worse for you. This is where those who think that the search for truth is an illusion end up. At the heart of this attitude is a profound intolerance of uncertainty and an unwillingness to accept that the less-than-perfect is better than nothing at all. Because we cannot know *everything* does not mean that we cannot know *something*. Our fallibility does not let us off the hook to pursue the truth as conscientiously as we can. As Francis Bacon, the sixteenth-century philosopher and politician, wrote:

> The inquiry of truth, which is the love-making or wooing of it, the knowledge of it, which is the presence of it, and the belief of the truth, which is the

enjoying of it, is the sovereign good of human nature.

∾ *Reverence for the Facts*

Science, at its best, has a reverence for the unknown and moves ahead by a process of trial and error. When we look at the way science works, the process is complex and often confusing, ambiguous, and misleading. My friends who are scientists love to prove themselves wrong! They know their need of each other for the sake of checks and balances. Walter Alvarez, professor of geology at the University of California at Berkeley, worked with his father on the question of why the dinosaurs became extinct. As he described their adventure in discovery, I couldn't help imagining the two of them working together on some huge crossword puzzle. Eventually, they came to the conclusion that it was caused by a meteor that struck the earth, a meteor so big that the dust cloud it made on impact blotted out the sun and sky. It took years of work and the critical cooperation (and skepticism) of a vast network of colleagues to come to this now widely accepted conclusion about the extinction of the dinosaurs. The process was worth it; a little bit of the crossword puzzle had been filled in. Still another truth was served by this patient attention to detail: the moral and inner truth of dedicated scholars doing good and honest work. Their own souls were being built in the process. They not only found out something about the world, they discovered something about themselves. Walter is not only a good scientist; he is someone you can trust.

There are many people working on the great crossword puzzle in various disciplines. In fact, all of us, to one degree or another, are called to have a reverence for facts. The wonderful puzzle of the world requires that all of us do our part because the scientific enterprise relies on a vast network of interdependence. I have two other friends who teach at the University of California at Berkeley, one a physicist and the other a geologist, who tell me of their collaborative work on thinking about the age of the universe and the long-term weather patterns of the planet. They float their theories, backed up by research and observation, in a critical community of their peers and wait for new information that will either corroborate or demolish their ideas.

This collaborative testing is true of every human enterprise and is also a cardinal rule of the spiritual life. None of us has to start from scratch. The pursuit of truth—even the most objective kind—is a deeply and unavoidably *social* enterprise. Furthermore, the pursuit of truth in one direction leads to truth in other dimensions. Both help build a community of trust. Reverence for middle C as middle C is the beginning of a journey that leads to truth in all its radiance.

There *are* truths other than naked facts to consider, such as moral and political questions about the distribution of resources and the application of scientific knowledge. In medicine we have made enormous scientific and technological advances, but deeper questions come into play when we have to think about who lives, who dies, and who decides. It is easy to see how truth—if we pursue it diligently—always leads to questions of *trust*. But it does more than that. Truth-telling actually *creates* a community of trust The world is more than a puzzle, more than a morass of problems to be negotiated. It is also a mystery in which we live and move and have our being. In the pursuit of truth, sometimes we will be puzzle solvers and at other times we will find ourselves in what appear to be intractable moral dilemmas. And undergirding us, if we see the world through the eyes of love and gratitude, will also be truth as a sustaining mystery.

As Lewis Lapham, the editor of *Harpers*, wrote in a recent edition of the magazine, "The truth isn't about the assimilation of doctrine or statistics, nor even about the discovery of termites in the wainscoting of the White House. It's about acquiring the courage of one's own thought, and if it's impossible to have courage without convictions, it's equally impossible to have convictions without knowledge and understanding." Acquiring the courage of one's own thought is essential to the human enterprise. Such courage requires convictions. And convictions without knowledge and understanding are worthless. The pursuit of truth has its own disciplines of accuracy and collaboration, of trust and humility. Truth and trust build community.

❧ *The Discipline of Truth-Telling*

As we have seen, when you move from puzzle to mystery you cannot help bumping into the issue of trust. But who or what can be entrusted with the truth? Remember John? There are *other* versions of John's life that are not as generous or as true as the one told by his friends and family. In fact, he lost many whom he thought were his friends, who abandoned him because he embarrassed them. They told stories about him—all of them technically "true"—that made John out as a lost soul and afforded them the opportunity to feel both concerned and superior.

Is a truth spoken with a motive to hurt really true? Where does truth-telling end and muck-raking begin? Truth-telling is hard work because it requires a discerning and loving heart as well as a respect for accuracy. It is small wonder that when it comes to truth-telling (whether we are solving part of the puzzle or moving deeper into mystery) we tend to avoid its disciplines, precisely because the road is hard. Most of us choose the easy way out. The truth is reduced to what most people around us believe. It is easier to go with the flow, follow the crowd.

Real truth-telling involves some uncomfortable admissions. My friend John had to be confronted with hard facts: his drinking and its effect on his family, his work, his life. He found that at the root of the search for truth is always a call to a change of life (conversion) and a renewed mind (repentance). When I seek the truth I have to be prepared for a revelation about myself, which may cause a revolution. I am tempted to return to the shadows when the light of truth shines directly on me and challenges me not only to tell the truth but somehow to *be* it as well. *Being* the truth involves sorting out memories and impressions of the past in order to live in the present without pretense.

We like to believe that when we speak the truth about the past it corresponds to an objective state of affairs. An old friend of mine used to say, "I know it's true. It's in my journal!" Most of us subscribe to this rudimentary, everyday view of truth as a means of describing the world factually. It is not to be dismissed: I want to live in a reliable world in which everyone is committed to *accuracy*. This is not only true when it comes to hard facts; it is just as true for the soft ones as well. Facts and their interpretation get blurred in our memories. How reliable are they? When I remember things I try not to edit anything out, but I know that a crude view of *this* equals *that* is not sufficient when it comes to doing justice to the past.

❧ The Truth of the Past

Often we experience a deep sadness when we think of the terrible truth of the unalterable past. Sometimes a deep grief overcomes us when beautiful memories shatter in hindsight because the remembered happiness fed not just on actual circumstances but on a promise that was not kept. We failed in some way to live up to our promise. We broke our word or betrayed another. We suddenly realize that the past was not as we remember it. We despair. We become angry. Truth becomes a matter of judgment and the judgment is against us. The past cannot be altered. Its truths are inexorable. That is why John spent a great deal of energy rewriting his history so that he could come out on top. And moving into the morass of recent history, what if the Serbs really did butcher my father and mother and my little sister? Nothing can change *that,* and now it is time that the Serbs got theirs. That is the seductive "truth" of revenge and retribution. The past must be taken care of.

Many experience the past as a burden, even a tragedy. When we experience life as a waste of time, we lose hope. As Jacob Needleman writes, "There is that in us which could give us an entirely different kind of future than the one we are trying to fabricate from our anxious imaginings."[5] He points out that the way we experience the passing of time depends entirely on the degree to which we are either seeking truth or pursuing a lie. It is because of our lies and self-deceptions that we suffer from spiritual starvation. What are we? What are we meant to be? Whom are we meant to serve? These are both faith questions and truth questions. The spiritual life is about beginning again, about rebirth, about God as a great incomprehensible presence within each one of us. We are not what we think we are. We are both more and less: more, because we are deeper and lovelier than we know; less, because we often inflate ourselves by power, money, or arrogance to compensate for our feared insignificance. As Needleman writes, "We squander our time because we do not remember the truth about ourselves or about the world in front of us."[6] When we pursue a lie, we are ruled by negative emotions: fear, guilt, self-pity, hurt feelings, anger, lovesickness. We nurse these feelings and become addicted to negativity, self-pity, and resentment. We even hug our guilt over trivial things.

How we live through time, then, will depend on our awareness of the truth in all its forms: as fact, as interpretation, as trust, and as community. The deeper we get into the subject of truth-telling, the more complex it becomes. Trust and forgiveness become important: I want to know not only whether it is raining outside but also that, when you *tell* me it's raining, you are to be trusted. To put it in terms of another age, I want to know if you are possessed by a true spirit. It is one thing for me to know whether it is raining outside and quite another for me to know if you are a trustworthy person. If I want to know the truth about you, I have to rely on your revealing something of your inner self. You might be telling me the truth but you might be lying. Conversation and interpretation are the tools of this kind of truth-telling, but they are notoriously tricky instruments.[7]

It is good, then, that we struggle for accuracy, but accuracy is not enough. We want truthfulness and sincerity, too. In the old wedding service the couple said to each other, "And thereto I plight thee my troth." I give you my truth, my word, my "me." I pledge you my fidelity. Truth, in this deepest sense, has something to do with love. Remember, *only love can be entrusted with the truth.* If you want to know the truth of my heart, you won't find out by using the same method you would use to see if it's raining outside. You will have to go deeper than the facts if you want to know the truth of who I am, and swim in the deep waters of interpretation. How we interpret each other will depend on the kind of language we speak and the inner dictionaries available to us. Who I am will be filtered through the grid of your hopes and fears. Who you are will be subject to the same filtering. It is not always pleasant, but there is no other way to fullness of life.

We know how notoriously difficult it is to interpret inner realities. Life has depths as well as surfaces. I cannot always depend on your being truthful. You might deliberately lie to me, or you might lie to me *intending* to tell me the truth. You might also lie to yourself, so the process gets complicated and demanding. The philosopher Ken Wilbur sums it up well: "Surfaces can be seen, but depths must be interpreted."[8] And when it comes to interpretation, there are bound to be disagreements and arguments. This is why history is always being rewritten. Historians have to be faithful to the facts, but they disagree as to the overarching story into which the facts might fit. John's friends had enough trouble in speaking what they thought was the truth about him. Think how much harder it is to write the truth about the actions of hundreds of people involved in the French Revolution, the Vietnam War, or the break-up of the Soviet Union.

When we move from the disciplines of history to interpreting our own history, we learn that truth-telling pushes us toward certain ways of acting in the world and away from others. We bump into questions of morality. People who speak the truth are expected to keep their word. They do not break promises. We can no more escape from moral judgments than escape from being human, so we need a moral compass we can trust.

When trust becomes a matter of doubt in human relations, something incalculable is lost. Think of our propensity for litigation and for throwing people in jail, for relying on legal controls to regulate personal life when only forgiveness and reconciliation will work. It is a sign not only of our lack of trust but also that there is no consensus as to the meaning of the words we use to interpret the world. Prenuptial agreements are surrogates for trust, as are strict rules of engagement in the workplace. One state has made a law that children should address their teachers as Sir or Ma'am; others want to set up the Ten Commandments in public places. Why? Because life falls apart when there are no shared stories embodying agreed-upon values. In Kansas, the school board has eliminated the teaching of evolution as a required science course; in a

Gallup poll sixty-eight percent of Americans said that it was all right to teach creationism alongside evolution.

These are among the many forces in the world that erode the conviction that each of us is responsible for our actions and therefore we are able to trust each other. We are more helpless than ever before the power of the pressures of society and its special interest groups. If I am to trust you and you are to trust me, both of us have to be reasonably confident that the other is responsible for his or her actions. Without that moral compass we are lost. A world of individuals who cannot trust one another is a form of hell.

∾ *Watch Your Language!*

No wonder, then, we are impatient with regard to issues of truth. We resist admitting that there are *levels* of truth (some truths are not as important as others) and find it annoying that something could be true on one level and not on another. We believe the myth that truths are unchanging, that truth is fate. This struggle became obvious when John's friends tried to interpret his life as an alcoholic, a husband, a father, and a businessman. We realized how dangerous the verb *to be* is, especially when we allow a minor—if significant—truth about someone (John *is* an alcoholic) to define reality. John *is* an alcoholic, but that is not *all* he is; to say so is a lie. The verb *to be* tends to act as a magnet drawing everything to itself: "John *is* a drunk." "Mary *is* a nag." "Susan *is* an angel." "Peter *is* a saint." Language is slippery, but we cannot help using metaphor, myth, and poetry to describe the world and our feelings about it. In moving from puzzle to morass to mystery, we push language to its limits.

It is no accident that early theologians thought of God as the Word. In God the Word and the Truth coincide. With us it is different. Theologian Charles Williams once pointed out that the word is either spiritual truth or verbal filth. Human beings can never quite do justice to the inner truth of things. Our speech is never completely accurate; in fact, we can say true things falsely, speak the literal truth and still be untrustworthy. "Actions speak louder than words," we say. The proper use of language is a godly thing, whereby words and actions are in complete harmony with each other. When we speak and mean what we say, and try to act on what we say and mean, we move closer to what we are meant to be. In our struggle to speak, do, and be the truth we learn humility and know our need for grace. Integrity, in the end, is a gift rather than an achievement.

Language, then, *forms* us rather than informs us. When it is corrupted, other corruptions follow. George Orwell's horror story *1984* is a parable about what happens when words are cut off from their true meanings. In Dante's *Inferno,* the deepest circle of hell is deceit and betrayal. The corruption of language means the breakdown of human relations. It is a form of forgery. When the currency of human interaction is counterfeit we are all lost. Words are our means of communication. Pollute our relationships with flattery and deceit, our language with lies and propaganda, our common life with the self-serving use of images, and what happens? We can no longer reach each other, and, what is worse, we lose touch with ourselves.

A friend of mine who was at West Point in 1945 wrote me recently about the academy's honor code, which stated, "We will neither lie, cheat nor steal or tolerate among us those who do." In his letter he remarked on how important this code was to the integrity of relationships:

> One of the most interesting things about having such a strong honor code is the way you have relationships with other people....I think there is a confidence people get when they realize that all of

their associates are telling the truth. This carries over into the Army where people are responsible for the lives of others and just expect the absolute truth as a normal condition of life. There is no telling how many lives have been saved by this tradition of complete truth.

What does it take for you to be truly at home with yourself, to be honored in your deepest self? How do you strive for the deeper truth without either being crippled by idealism or inflated with self-importance? We do not have to give up on our ideals, provided we know our need for forgiveness. Truth-telling functions rather like a home-coming. "Come home! All is forgiven!" Pretense is at an end. The Greek word for truth is *aletheia*—it has the word *lethe* in the middle of it, the river of forgetfulness. Truth-telling uncovers what has been repressed and forgotten. It is a form of restoration for the soul.

The philosopher Søren Kierkegaard wrote of the "wound of possibility." Being human involves our bearing a kind of open wound, the sign of a future over which we have no control and in which the choices we make have unforeseen and unintended consequences. The wound of possibility teaches us some important lessons. We are not as important as we think we are. We are not the center of events. In the end we will die. In the light of these truths, how do we *choose* to see the world? What will bring us integrity and purpose? What drives us—gratitude, resent-ment, fear, compassion? What is our ruling passion? Is it our desire to be noticed and the rage we feel when we are rendered invisible and insignificant? Is it our thirst for recognition?

The longing for truth has to do with being recognized, desired, and loved. God sees, recognizes, and loves us. This is how one tradition has tried to speak of the Absolute Truth, as sustaining Love. The search for truth and truthfulness, for trust and integrity, means we are willing to seek out the root of our longing to be in relationships that recognize and respect us. The fact that we can count on middle C always being middle C is a sign of the betrothing that holds the universe together.

∾

Chapter 3

Finding a Story Faithful to the Facts

Facts are like fish in the sea—what you catch is what you're looking for.[1]

When Herbert Spencer, a late-nineteenth-century philosopher, wrote his autobiography, he called in all his letters and used only those passages that confirmed his own view of himself and then destroyed the rest. This is what most of us would like to do if given the chance to create a life in which all the inconvenient bits are edited out. What makes us *choose* a particular story, a particular narrative, by which to interpret our experience and not another? Is it all a matter of psychology and upbringing? Is it sufficient to blame or praise our parents, or is there a way of looking at and being in the world that is indelibly and peculiarly ours?

One of the daughters in Mary Gordon's *The Other Side,* a novel about several generations of an Irish-American family, is an ex-nun with a definite lens through which she sees the world. In her working life, "she moved into administration saying she was 'burnt out.' But in fact she'd never caught fire." The woman has a talent for finding fault, thinking herself on the side of the poor who, in reality, irritate her. She copies the mean-spirited people from her childhood and early training who had taught her to *choose* bitterness as the lens through which she looked at life. Therefore the narrative she chooses of how the world works is one of revenge. "She'd seen them thrive on judgment," Gordon writes,

> finding in it nutrition, healing, the reward for hours of exhaustion and for years of self-control. Refusing alcohol (they saw its devastation all around them), they filled themselves on judgment, and then gave it out as calmly and with as much confidence as if they nursed the people whom they judged.[2]

Why choose one attitude to life over another? Surely some choices are not only better (from a practical point of view) but also *truer* than others? Which story we choose can be a matter of life and death.

At the end of William Golding's novel *Lord of the Flies*, which tells the story of a group of boys who are shipwrecked on a desert island and revert to barbarism, their leader Ralph is running for his life. The boys-turned-savages are screaming for his blood, for he is to be sacrificed to the stinking corpse that has become their god, the Lord of the Flies. Ralph manages to reach the beach where a naval officer stands on the sand, and at the sight of a figure of authority from the "civilized" world the boys begin to come to their senses. Then Golding asks a terrible question: while the naval officer rescued the children from their own terrible violence, who will rescue the adults? Golding implies that because the boys had no sustaining narrative and no moral compass to guide them, they had to invent one that, horrendous as it was, gave them a sense of purpose and meaning.[3]

Meaning requires narrative, but which story fits the bill and gives the best account of the wide range of human experience? How are we to *interpret* all the feelings and events of our lives? How do we find a story that is faithful to all that we have experienced? Can there be only one true interpretation or are there many?

We have already discovered that there are two conflicting meanings to the word "truth." Some affirm that truth is knowable in the ordinary sense of the word, while others affirm that we are pilgrims to and of it. For pilgrims, truth is not something to be wrenched from intractable material. Our relationship to it is more like that of a lover than a master. In fact, mastery is the last thing we can do with the truth. Appreciation of mystery is the key—mystery not as a last resort "explanation," but as the container of all our explorations.

As the philosopher Diogenes Allen writes, "When we treat other people as objects subordinate to our goals, their mystery has no effect on us. The larger mystery into which genuine personal encounter can lead us never becomes open to us."[4] Sometimes we use force to protect us from the mystery of others. Our desire for control cuts us off from depths of truth that come to us only when we are available to others. The necessity of being available to others in order to achieve a deeper kind of truth understandably makes us nervous. We take refuge in "facts," in the hard truths of science. Facts, after all, are more reliable than people. Middle C is always middle C. Better to stay with what we know than leap into the abyss of the unknown and untried.

But even the truths of science are not quite as "hard" as they used to be. Theories are often in dispute and the models of the universe change from time to time (from *machine* to *mind* to *living organism,* for example) Yet, as we have seen, the conclusions of science seem pretty solid compared to the truths of history. It is no wonder that science has been so revered in the past century. It appears dependable, certain, and true. But science is limited, and, at its best, poses questions that it cannot answer. It can no more explain the universe than a clock, left to itself, can tell the time.[5] In the end, truth needs a story.

❧ One Thing After Another

What happens when stories dry up and there is no interpretive key to unlock the door of meaning, no way of sifting through the morass of information in front of us? Where are we to find some organizing principle? When life is simply one thing after another, with no connecting narrative, what are we to do? Or when life is one thing *instead* of another? The poet Philip Larkin asked, "And what remains when disbelief has gone?" What happens when there aren't any certainties left to undermine? Cynics find themselves out of a job. What happens when people have nothing from which to lapse? People used to say, "I was raised a Catholic, a Protestant, a Jew, but now I have left all that behind." They affirm that they once had a reference point, something—true north—by which they could take their bearings. They were able to locate themselves in a tradition and a story. Many people, of course, experienced the traditions and stories of their childhood as enslaving, and need to break free from the crippling narrative learned from the community into which they were born. We should take care what stories we tell ourselves about ourselves, and yet the point is, we cannot do without a story of some sort. The facts demand it.

Much of our trouble with the truth-claims of religion is due to a misunderstanding. We think that religion must be either right or wrong, true or false. But this is to fail to see the "story" as a living organic reality, capable of metamorphosis. Even my skeptical friends found a negative pole star in an "unchanging" Christianity. It was always there and it was always *dependably* wrong! I remember an atheist acquaintance being furious with me when I told him that I did not believe that the unbaptized went to hell. He wanted me to believe in such stupidities so that he could feel comfortable in his unbelief. What remains when disbelief has gone? What is left? Credulity, certainly. Perhaps a retreat into the imagined, perfect past.

Faith in technology fills the gap for some who have lost their bearings. It enables them to believe in a utopian future. Others are attracted to rigid belief-systems that eliminate any traces of uncertainty. Literalism—a flat, one-dimensional take on life—is a popular option not confined to religious people: it is a characteristic of some people who would call themselves agnostics or even athe-ists. Rigid certainty based on a literalistic view of the world is as attractive to liberals as it is to conservatives. When we run out of old certainties, we find new ones. What we need are stories that are always open to revision and are hospitable to a wider spectrum of human experi-ence. Literalism is the enemy of truth in this deepest sense because its lens is too narrow.

Furthermore, it is all very well to assemble the pieces of the puzzle, but how should they be arranged? Is there an overall picture and, if so, what is it? One of the early Christians accused the heretics of taking all the bits and pieces of the life and work of Christ and assembling them into the head of a fox instead of the face of Jesus. Imagine two people, each with the same number of pieces of stone and the same number of colors to make a mosaic. The ingredients are identical but the results will be radically different. So it is with the building blocks of truth. The pieces matter, but so does the *arrangement* of the pieces.

∾ *Exercises in Truth-Telling*
It is one thing, therefore, to assemble the facts but quite another to find a story that is faithful to the facts. This is why texts and stories are important. The rabbis estab-

lished a method of endless argument over the meaning of texts. Texts were central but so was the *debate* about their meaning and status. No one has the last word. Texts provide the maps we need to make the journey, but they are not the journey itself any more than a menu is the actual meal. We stumble into the mystery of ourselves and find multiple meanings. The deeper we go, the more frustrated we can become. As we learn to trust the journey, we can also become more content with the kind of knowledge that is a not-knowing, an expectant waiting for the truth to appear. Life is a kind of dance and we have to learn the steps.

One of the hardest exercises in truth-telling are the arts of biography and history. What is the truth about the Civil War? How do you explain an Adolf Hitler? What is the significance of Jesus? What is the true meaning of Islam? Was the ethnic cleansing in the Balkans really religiously motivated or was it simply a matter of land and economics? What is the truth about Napoleon? Ask a group of Americans about the truth of Franklin D. Roosevelt and you will hear passionately held and opposite views about his administration and the New Deal.

If biography and history are difficult to think about, how much harder is *autobiography*? It was hard enough to come up with "the truth about John." But what is the truth about you? Who would you trust to tell it? Underneath this question often lurks a deep anxiety. If you knew all there was to know about me, would you still love me?

Some time ago I went through a divorce, with all the shame, guilt, and sense of failure that such a process entails. No matter what I did, someone was going to be hurt. How was I to interpret my experience of failure? As a priest I have always preached to those who have lost their way rather than those who seem to have, as a friend of mine wrote to me recently, "all their spiritual ducks in a row." My friend—also divorced—went on to ask why I didn't address issues of separation and divorce directly in my sermons. I don't like undigested autobiography in the pulpit, but my friend had a point. How do you address the burden of past mistakes? Where is the truth to be found?

My divorced friend had found himself living in a nightmare, a character in a story written by someone else. So he asked me to see my separation and divorce not only as an area of my personal life, but as something that affects millions of people. When I shared something of my story with him, it helped him get out of one story into another. The morass of "facts" of my divorce and what led up to it were piled up all around me, but how was I to assemble them into a story that wasn't merely self-serving but true? Jacob Needleman's admonition in *Time and the Soul* came to my mind, where he wrote, "Our relationship to time is what it is because we lie to ourselves about what we are and what we can do and we hide from ourselves what we are meant to be and what we are meant to serve."[6] I had to remind myself over and over again that the deep truth of the spiritual life is that we can begin again, we can be born anew. This is central to everyone's story.

Thus, the interpretation of the self depends on the prism through which you look at life. When we probe the past we are humbled by the weight of human experience that has preceded us. We reach for the truth, but who would claim to have finally found it? We are always pilgrims. There will be some people (I hope not many) in the world for whom I will dependably remain a bastard and terribly wrong. But even this belief, another friend reminded me, is a sign of arrogance. Who am I to say that those who judge me are incapable not only of changing their minds but also of forgiveness and reconciliation? The art is first to face the dark truths about oneself and second, to know where to *place* them in the story. If you place them

too far away in the background you slip into self-deception. If you place them too much in the foreground you
risk distortion. The question is which is greater, your sin
or God's love? What is the most real thing about you—the
fact that you messed up your marriage or the fact that you
were created for joy and delight? As William Langland,
the late-medieval poet, wrote, "And all the wickedness in
the world that man might work or think is no more to the
mercy of God than a live coal dropped into the sea."

Remember: In this poor world, *only love can be
entrusted with the truth.* Who you believe yourself to be
will be determined by the way you tell the story, not only
of your life but of Life with a capital L. Truth-telling is not
only a matter of accuracy but of *placement.* We not only
want to know what is true but where a particular truth fits
in the larger scheme of things. It is not much use knowing
lots of little truths if we do not have an overarching vision
into which they belong. We also have to be careful of volume control: sometimes an incident long in the past takes
up a disproportionate amount of space and makes so
much noise that nothing else can be seen or heard. One of
the spiritual tasks for the truth-teller is to develop a grid
into which the various truths fit. What kind of narrative
will do justice to the facts?

If truth is a question of the choice of narratives, it is
also a matter of proportion, of hierarchy. The word "hierarchy" has had a bad time lately, suggesting as it does the
exercise of power over others that is often associated with
male dominance. But the word has a benign or neutral
meaning, too, having to do with the way things are
ordered and how they fit together. In the middle ages people thought in terms of a great order of being, a chain
from the simplest to the most complex. No matter where
a creature was in the chain, it had its own particular excellence. For example, a stone might be low in the chain of
being but possess strength and durability not enjoyed by a

finch, which in its turn displayed other qualities of song, delicacy, and movement. *Truth is a matter of relationship.*

We have a double task, then, of being as clear and accurate as we can in our truth-telling but also of knowing how the various truths *relate* to one another. That relationship will depend on the story we tell and where, in the scheme of things, we *place* all the actors in the drama.

During the impeachment proceedings against President Clinton, I suggested to moralistic friends on both sides of the issue that they imagine every character in the drama to be in Dante's inferno, with its narrowing circles of damnation. Since my friends were worried that someone was going to get away with something, I asked them where would they place all the characters in relation to each other in the ever-narrowing circles of hell. Where would President Clinton be in relation to Linda Tripp? Would Kenneth Starr be higher or lower than Monica Lewinsky? Where would the members of Congress find themselves? It wasn't a very serious exercise but it did show the difficulties in finding the truth behind the facts, of finding a story into which all the facts *faithfully* fitted.

In the spiritual life, we struggle with the same kinds of questions. Accuracy demands that we try not only to assemble the facts, but also to discern how they are related one to another. For example, how is my love of ice cream related to my love of reading? What is the right ordering of my loving? In the chain of my attitudes and emotions, where do fear and self-preservation belong?

Being committed to the truth involves a process of continual conversion. It is about the reordering of priorities, of refining our vision of truth so that in the end we choose the clarity of love over the distortions of fear. As I grow spiritually, can I discern that compassion, mercy, tenderness, and generosity are on the side of truth rather than judgmentalism, resentment, and vindictiveness? Am I able to say why? I could only account for my choice of compassion over resentment by reference to a story larger and more generous than my own.

◌ *Appealing to Stories*

We all make truth claims and do so by appealing to stories. Nations as well as individuals need some kind of story to explore what they think is the truth. One of the most difficult stories to tell in recent times is that of the Balkans. That saga has been going on for centuries. At its center is the martyr complex of the Serbs. We need to be careful in invoking a people as an example, but there is such a thing as a Serbian myth and it is alive and well. This six-hundred-year-old national myth teaches the Serbs that their past, present, and future consists of endless cycles of Christ-like passions and resurrections. This "truth about Serbia" began in 1389 in Kosovo. On the eve of a great battle an eagle swooped down from heaven holding a book in its claws, which told Serbian Prince Lazar that he would have to choose between a heavenly martyr's victory or an earthly one over the Ottomans. He chose martyrdom and hence martyrdom for the nation, too. The myth goes something like this: the deep spiritual truth of martyrdom is that whenever you lose on the battlefield you win a moral victory. Only the Serbs know what real suffering is, and suffering means that you are right. It is also a license to kill. Suffering and victimization become the key to interpreting everything, the truth through which all truths are filtered.

Vuk Draskovic, the former deputy Prime Minister of Yugoslavia, wrote in his novel *Prayer,* "There are not only individual martyrs but also nation-martyrs, those that are always found guilty by somebody and apparently bear Golgotha as their eternal sentence. Christ was crucified for three hours only, but some nations never descend from the Cross." Journalist Victoria Clark, touring Serbian Orthodox monasteries with a Serb friend in 1997, asked him to account for the war crimes. Unlike western democracies, in Orthodox countries a wider gap exists between the best and the worst, differences that are exaggerated in times of war. "So I would expect that if Serbia has war criminals...then she has some real saints as well." Victoria Clark wondered if he thought it was fair to slaughter thousands of non-Orthodox on the chance of hatching a few Orthodox saints! No doubt it was, was the reply.[7]

Two principles emerge in our pursuit of truth and in truth's pursuit of us.

   What you think is the truth depends on what you believe.

   What you think is the truth depends on who you think you are.

What we believe about what it is to be human makes a difference with regard to the way we arrange the facts of life and turn them into a story. This is because "the truth that matters to people is not factual truth but moral truth; not a narrative that tells *what* happened but a narrative that explains *why* it happened and who is responsible."[8] What is my "truth," I ask myself? "I might not be much but I am, thank God, *not....*" You can make up your own list of *nots* that feed your personal myth of who you are. Such myths need no evidence. They feed the deep sadness and rage within as we look for a "true" story to tell us how we came to be the way we are.

If you are trying to find a story to do justice to the facts, consider the mystery of freedom. Many national and personal stories have to do with liberty. Most of us have a very thin view of freedom: for us liberty means doing what we want to do when we want to do it. We exercise our freedom in going to Burger King instead of McDonalds or buying a Ford instead of a Chevy. But underneath all our choices is an unnerving question. Am I choosing in such a way that accords with who I truly am? Do my choices move me toward or away from integrity? Do my actions make me more "me" or do I diminish myself by what I do? Just as there is a higher truth so there is a higher freedom—the freedom to be who we truly are. Liberty is an arduous discipline.

What are the stories of liberation? What narrative does justice to our longing for integrity and joy? *Choosing* the prism through which we see the world is a matter of faith. Which prism gives the truest view? Once you have chosen, you will find moral clarity. Your moral vision may be repellent to others but for you the way ahead is clear. Hitler knew the "truth" and was frighteningly clear about his mission to preach it. Choosing the lens through which we see the world is a matter of life and death. But it isn't a game of Russian roulette, a matter of sheer chance. Faith as it relates to truth must be reasonable—that is, capable of including all the facts that we can assemble, all the horror and glory of human experience.

Why should we care? Even if truth-telling is a matter of accuracy, proportion, and hierarchy, what difference does it make? This question is nowhere more poignant than in those accounts of concentration camp commandants listening to Beethoven and Schubert in the evenings while during the day they ordered or permitted atrocities. More recently, film director Ermanno Olmi, during the presentation of a letter by Pope John Paul II to artists at the Vatican in April of 1999, said in an interview printed in *Italy Daily,* "The night before the start of NATO bombardments in Yugoslavia they were showing Roberto Benigni's *Life is Beautiful* in Belgrade, and everyone was going there to be moved by this representation of the sacredness of life. So I ask myself how much art really counts for in people's lives."

My response is to ask another question: "What is the alternative?" Novelist Walker Percy wrote somewhere that artists and people of the Spirit are often like the canaries people used to send down coal mines to see if the air was sweet and safe enough to breath. Some people are like that. They are sent ahead of us to test the air. And some of them suffer greatly on our behalf so that we can breathe. It may sound grim to affirm (also with Walker Percy) that the person of faith is an ex-suicide, the one who has faced death and said to herself, "I may as well live!" She can get up in the morning and laugh and go to work because she doesn't have to.

A story may help. A friend of mine is a Vietnam vet. He does not often talk about his experiences of combat all those years ago and it is hard to imagine this successful businessman flying into the uncertainties and dangers of war. But at a restaurant in Santa Fe recently he and the waiter discovered that they both had served in Vietnam and shared similar experiences. Once you got into the battle zone, uniforms were set aside and new rules applied. Survival was the name of the game and when it was your turn to get out of that particular inferno you were apt to point out to those who were replacing you (as you passed by them at the airport) that not all of them would be returning. The waiter loved life and he said to my friend, "I just can't explain what this time in Vietnam did to me. As I see it—the deal is this. You wake up! You're alive! You win!" When my friend told me the story I couldn't help remembering what one of the monks who taught me told me about prayer. Prayer is a daily placing oneself on the threshold of death. It helps us anticipate and participate in our dying, and this is good news because it also means we participate in the new life of the Spirit. The deal is this. You wake up! You're alive! You win!

This happens to be a story about being fully alive but let's also remember the power of some of the stories we tell ourselves about ourselves. One small incident can change what we believe to be true. The daughter of a former East German diplomat tells of how her father defected during the Stalinist regime. His defection deeply embarrassed his daughter, but she was touched by the incident that turned him away from Communism. "One night—in Moscow—he heard the screams." That was all it took for the story he had been telling himself about the truth of the world to unravel. Communism as a binding narrative fell apart. Many of our binding narratives are just as frail.

Remember, "Surfaces can be seen, but depths must be interpreted." It is now time to go into those depths, where our journey is filled with even more hazards than our exploring truth-as-fact. Truth is also fiction. Truth is a story. And stories lie as well as tell the truth. We shall have to take care.

ꞷ *What you think is the truth depends on what you believe.*

ꞷ *What you think is the truth depends on who you think you are.*

part two

Truth as Fiction

Chapter 4

The Craft of
Truth-Telling

*Life is an art, with disciplines and skills that have to
be learned if its truth is to be fully appreciated.*

A t school I was never any good at sports, but I did
flourish in the school's dramatic society. It soon
became clear to me that we are all actors playing various
parts (by turns, tragic and comic) in a drama of infinite
variety. We cannot avoid playing a role. Sometimes we are
the audience; sometimes the victim; sometimes the righteous judge or the wronged lover. The roles change,
although some of us so prefer certain roles in life that we
play little else: the martyred mother, the angry father, the
rebellious child. In my school's dramatic society, I learned
something of the mysterious relationship between role and
identity. If we play a role long enough we can become it,
and so we find it hard at the end of our performance to
take off the costume, remove the make-up, and allow ourselves the right (as scary as it is sometimes) to stand naked,
even for a few moments.

47

It might seem strange to place the theatrical next to the tasks of self-knowledge and identity, but there is nothing quite like taking on a role in a play for helping you to get to know yourself. Drama is narrative, and as we have seen, truth is inextricably bound up with narrative. Which story shall we tell? Which version? What play are we currently in and what is our part? When I was growing up, the choice of the play and the assignment of parts all seemed arbitrary and unfair, based on seniority and not on ability. Who got the big and important parts and who got the one-liners and walk-ons was based on the hierarchy of the school. In a rigid class system, casting was a matter of caste. From where I waited in the wings, a good part didn't appear to rely on skill or competence.

But I soon began to realize that while the drama of life appeared a hit-and-miss affair, I had the power to choose to make the best of it. There were things I could learn of the craft of acting—standing still on stage, for one thing, speaking clearly for another. I remember a hilarious school production of *Macbeth*. I was acknowledged as one of the better actors in the dramatic society but I was given the very minor part of Ross, whose one scene is to tell Macduff that his wife and children had been murdered. I had not learned the old saying, "There are no small roles, only small actors," and I would not have believed it had I known it. On the opening night I marched onstage and uttered my lines, and Macduff's response to the devastating news brought screams of laughter from the audience. It was the way he delivered the line, "What? All? All my pretty chickens and their dam in one fell swoop! What? All?" The words came out in a kind of cockney wail. I froze at the laughter, fled to the back of the stage, and held my head in my hands as if in grief. I learned something that night about humor, humiliation, and limitation.

The French essayist and philosopher Montaigne wrote about human failure and inconsistency as we all seek to play our roles in life. In his essay entitled "Of the Inconsistency of our Action," Montaigne wrote about the many faces of the soul, including its inconsistency and frailty, saying, "All the contradictions are to be found in me, according as the wind turns and changes." If we are to move ahead in our pilgrimage, we will have to give up our longing for consistency. What is the truth about you in the light of all the discordance and unsteadiness within you?

Allow yourself to think about your self as a work-in-progress, a work of art. We learn about being human by imitation and repetition. Art's mystery lies in the fact that every repetition or performance is unique and unrepeatable. Just like you. Allow for the possibility of revelation.

Early on, then, through acting in the school's dramatic society, I learned three things that have shaped my understanding of the pursuit of truth.

   Life is an art, with disciplines and skills that have to be learned if its truth is to be fully appreciated.

   The world is full of resonance and presence, which shows us that there are layers of truth, depths for which we have to wait to reveal themselves.

   The world is essentially something I share with others. It is social. There is no strictly private reality.

Being human is like learning a craft, and becoming part of a tradition. We are in it together. Salvation is social. Think about any skill you may have acquired—baseball, quilting, cooking, music-making. These skills are not acquired through the democratic process but by authority and discipline; we learn by paying attention, by listening, by practice. Why should the art of truth-telling be any different?

We are all actors and there are lines to learn, moves to remember, costumes to try on, and a grinding rehearsal schedule that leads to a great event of the theater, which is the revelation of one part of the truth.

❧ The Craft of Being Human

We did not emerge from the womb fully formed. It takes a long time to make a human being. An older view called education "the formation of character." We had to learn about life through trial and error. In the past people were more conscious than we are of the importance of passing their traditions on to their children, often through texts that were learned by heart. Carved around the fourteenth-century font in the parish church of Bradley in Lincolnshire, England, are these words:

> Pater Noster, Ave Maria, Criede,
> Leren the childe yt is nede.

"Children should be taught / The Our Father, the *Ave Maria,* and the Creed." How many of us who are Christians have taught our children the Lord's Prayer and the creed, let alone the *Ave Maria?* Learning by rote on its own is of little use, but it is also easy to undervalue and even deride a useful exercise in memory. It is good for us to have some "texts" buried in the mind and heart to feed on and bump up against. Children assimilate a great deal from television; mine have the ability to sing many a jingle from an oft-repeated ad. We cannot help having minds furnished with something, so we might as well see to it that they are as well furnished as possible.

Peter Brook, one of the great theater directors of this century, writes about issues of integration of mind, body, and spirit as part of the discipline of not only being an actor but of being human.[1] To be truly ourselves requires a balance of mind, heart, and body. Like the contemplative disciplines of all the great religious traditions, acting requires radical attentiveness. This wakefulness applies to the function and role of the audience in the theater as well. For the audience is not passive, but should provide an awakened *presence*. Brook tells us that in front of an audience the actor cannot allow himself to be "any-old-how"—that is, unintegrated and unawake. The *truth* of a great performance requires the disciplines of attentiveness and practice: "For an actor's intention to be perfectly clear, with intellectual alertness, true feeling and balanced and tuned body, the three elements—thought, emotion, body—must be in perfect harmony."[2]

Much of the time we live "any-old-how," moving through our days on automatic pilot until suddenly life grabs our attention and some part of us—the mind, the heart, or the body—wakes up. When we are taking an exam or engaged in intense conversation, for example, our minds will be alert but our bodies will not. If, on the other hand, we are with someone who is in distress, we are likely to be kind and attentive in our feelings, but our thoughts may be adrift or confused and the same with our bodies. Whereas if we are driving a car, the entire body may well be mobilized, but the head, left to itself, can drift into "any-old-how" thoughts. Brook's point is that it is rare that all three "parts" of us—body, thoughts, and feelings—are working together. We tend to think of truth residing only in the head, but there is moral and emotional truth, too.

Remember the words of Ignatieff:

 ∾ *The truth that matters to people is not factual truth but moral truth; not a narrative that tells what happened but a narrative that explains why it happened and who is responsible.*

Brook suggests that there are disciplines for this important truth-bearing work of integration. Actors do all sorts of exercises in preparation for a role or a rehearsal:

breathing and body-work. Repetition. I remember hearing that actor John Gielgud would repeat a difficult word over and over again not so much to learn it as to build up the muscles in his mouth so that he could say it more easily. There are also exercises involving yelling and screaming, exercises with balls and sticks to practice coordination with others, exercises in speeding up and slowing down. What is it all for? Brook suggests that the goal for the actor is to find a panic-free emptiness within so that she may make room for the role and give it a chance to blossom.

We too are invited to give up our mental constructions of the truth and to allow for the panic-free emptiness within that leads to revelation. To reach this state we have body-work to help get rid of wasteful tensions and habits. That is why exercise is important for all of us; it is one of the spiritual disciplines that will open us up to the unlimited possibilities of emptiness. That is why taking time off for recreation and retreat is important. But these disciplines do not come cheap. Entering our emptiness and waiting in the dark stirs up resistance and fear, as Brook writes:

> At once one tries to fill it so as to get away from the fear, so as to have something to say or do. It takes real confidence to sit still or to stay silent. A large part of our excessive, unnecessary manifestations come from a terror that if we are not somehow signaling all the time that we exist, we will in fact no longer be there.[3]

Another lesson:

> ∾ *Truth-telling requires the allowing for a panic-free emptiness within so that the imagination can play.*

This necessity for a panic-free emptiness helps us understand, in part, what we mean by truth coming to us as artful fiction. Each of us has to find a role for ourselves.

∾ Building a Character

I was ordained a priest over thirty years ago. I did not really know what I was doing, although I had some ideas and some models. I still had to make it up as I went along. Like one of Brook's actors, I discovered that "what one calls 'building a character' is in fact fabricating a plausible counterfeit."[4] This idea is easy to misunderstand. Here I am not talking about hypocrisy and deliberate deception, but about the way the mystery of human personality grows and develops. We try on many costumes before we know who we truly are. Brook's advice is to wake us up to this fact and accept it as a way of being in the world.

The dangerous person is not the one who is acting a part, but the one who is acting a part and doesn't know it. It is not so much a choice between the sincere and the hypocritical as between those who know that they are playing a role and those who do not. I was once with a group of friends that included one of the most generous-hearted men I know, Ram Dass. When I kept on complaining about what was going on in my life, Ram Dass let me finish and then, with a broad grin, said, "Alan, enjoy the play!" It was the perfect response. I had made my life into a little drama without knowing it. This simple comment knocked me off my perch, made me laugh, reduced the fear, and allowed for emptiness. A few years later, Ram Dass suffered a stroke. He has not fully recovered but is able to speak, and in our most recent conversation I asked him what play he thought we were all in. He said something like, "The name of the game we are in is called 'Being at one with the Beloved.'" For him, life was and is a love story. Ram Dass is truly a man who makes space for the Beloved by allowing a panic-free emptiness inside.

Waiting in this emptiness allows our true form to appear. It is a fearful and wonderful thing to be a human being. The theological way of expressing this truth is to say that we are made, individually and collectively, in the image of God. This is the deepest truth about all of us. The divine is our true form, beyond our grasp and yet in our flesh. Every day and a thousand times a day we either assist in the birth of our selves or abort our souls.

Institutions help or hinder us in our being open to the true form. They are either bearers of deadly traditions or of the lively Tradition. I think of the church as rather like a theater director who is tempted to stage the play before the first day of rehearsal. It is understandable. The church has archives of wonderful material, a basement full of scenery, but it also has archives that need to be brought out to the light and burned, such as its terrible certainties, its past teaching on the fate of suicides and the unbaptized, its justification of slavery and the subjugation of women, its defense of racism, and its paranoia about sexuality.

I like the image of the theater because it can help us see that narratives can be revised and even rejected. New interpretations are always possible. As a way of personal and communal truth-telling, the theater brings acting and narrative together. It insists on three important connections: the vital links between actors and their inner life, their fellow-actors, and their audience. They tell us of the importance of such connections in our own lives. In order to tell the truth I need a deep connection with my own inner life, a respect for those with whom I am closely associated, and a commitment to building a community of free people. If I am not present and awake to you and you are as inattentive as I am, we are both failing in our obligation to each other to tell the story in all its fullness and truth. I also need to be in touch with the wealth of stories and traditions that my immediate community has available in its treasure-house.

Brook pays attention to those places in the world where great stories are told over and over again. The great storytellers he has heard in tea houses in Afghanistan and Iran recall ancient myths with much joy, but also with inner gravity. At every moment they open themselves up to their audiences, not to please them, but to share with them the qualities of a sacred text. Truth-telling in a community means being able to live in two worlds at the same time: the world of here-and-now and the world of the text. This listening, paying attention to each other *and* learning to act together on the same stage is how we create our world. This is another aspect of our sharing in the divine. To be human is to be a creator as well as a creature—to be a character in a play or story *and* a storyteller at the same time.

It sounds more difficult than it really is because we do much of what is required of us instinctively. When we watch a great performance, say, of *King Lear,* we learn something of what we do automatically in the world. We watch Lear and his youngest daughter, Cordelia, interrelate as truthfully as possible as king and daughter. But there is even more going on than this, because the actors, if they are good, carry us along, too. They model for us what we struggle to do when we try to live truthfully. They reveal the triple relationship to one's self, to the other, and, in our case, to the larger world. I also find it illuminating that one of the early traditions of the theater were the medieval mystery plays, which sought to understand the task of truth-telling as sharing in a great mystery.

One play that speaks particularly to the American soul is Arthur Miller's *Death of a Salesman.* The salesman Willy Loman committed suicide because the dream that once drove him lost its magic. As the little group gathers around his grave, his older son speaks the now-famous line, "He never knew who he was." Human unhappiness springs from a faulty diagnosis of the human condition.

His neighbor reflects, "And for a salesman there's no rock bottom to the life....He's a man way out there in the blue, riding on a smile and a shoeshine. And when they start not smiling back, that's an earthquake."

One can almost smell the sulfurous fire of the private hell of the person whose smile is never returned, whose longings are always aborted, whose hopes turn to ashes. Truth in this sense is knowing who we are, and knowing who we are involves knowing what play we are in or what play we need to get out of. It involves being aware that we are playing a role and that we have choices as to the roles we play and, if we are stuck in a social role, the *way* we play it. Knowing what play we are in helps, as does knowing the nature of the game of love that is our profoundest activity.

Robertson Davies' novel *Murther and Walking Spirits* is about a forty-four-year-old journalist ("Gil" Gilmartin) who is murdered right at the beginning of the story by his wife's lover. In a sort of purgatorial film festival, his spirit has to review the lives of his ancestors. Gilmartin's "history" takes him only as far back as the connections he had with his ancestors in the eighteenth century, but it is far enough for him to realize how deeply connected he is to everyone. Life is both a festival and a nightmare of mutuality and reciprocity. Gilmartin even discovers compassion for those who have made him who he was. When he thinks of their "courage and resource, loyalty even to the point of self-destruction, crankiness and meanness, despair and endurance," he feels not only admiration and pity but love. Why love? Because he knew more about them than he reckoned they had ever known about themselves.

Imagine someone knowing you better than you know yourself and finding you lovable! We barely know the truth about ourselves. If we did, we would behave differently. Gilmartin confesses,

It is as if my heart has been painfully enlarged, and in this swollen heart I must find a place for all that I have seen of my forebears, their vanities, their cruelties, their follies, which were, at least in part, explained and made to seem inevitable because of their circumstances. And in addition to these, something splendid—the stuff of life, indeed. Will the world that I no longer share think of me with love?[5]

When I die, will the world that I no longer share think of me with love? Can my heart be enlarged so as to widen its sympathies? Have I the depth of imagination to see something splendid struggling in the life of every human being, even the most wicked? When I find myself in a spiritual crisis, when I cannot control events, when I feel powerless and frightened, when I sometimes feel as if I've learned nothing, how do I move out of this terrifying void?

Novelist William Gass confesses, "I know of nothing more difficult than knowing who you are, and then having the courage to share the reasons for the catastrophe of your character with the world. Anyone honestly happy with himself is a fool. (It is not a good idea to be terminally miserable with yourself either.)"[6] The spiritual life is all about the emerging of a shaping self in the light of the stories celebrated and repeated by a community of faith. Living in community is discovering that we are jointly human. Only a fool isn't worried about the future; only a foolish pessimist would give up on the world. Pessimism is a seductive form of self-absorption—a trap for the unwary. The question is whether we believe not so much in God (in the first instance) as in the reality of other people. Do any of us really have a separate existence outside ourselves? Reality is social. Being is communion. That is the truth.

A rabbi once asked his students, "How can you tell when day is breaking?" One of them replied, "It's when

you look in the orchard and you can just make out the difference between a pear tree and an apple tree."

"No, that's not the answer," said the rabbi. Another
pupil said, "It's when you're looking down the road and
you can tell whether the animal ahead is a dog or a fox."

"That's not the answer either," said the rabbi. "Light
comes when you look into the eye of another human being
and know that he or she is your brother or your sister.
Until you can do that, it is *always* night, no matter what
time of day it is!"

What stories do you return to over and over again to
make sense of your life? What story, do you think, does
justice to the facts? What play are you currently in? How
long has it been running? Is the show still alive? What role
are you playing? Is your part fresh or a little stale? Is it
time you got out of the present drama? What is my
drama? Joyful and grateful reparation in the second half
of life.

∾

Chapter 5

Stories That Hold Us Together

The truth that matters to people is not factual truth, but moral truth—not a narrative that tells what happened, but one that explains why it happened and who is responsible.

We know the destructive power of some family, national, and religious stories. The place where I work sometimes feels like a refugee camp for people running away from the dark narratives of their past. The horror stories are from all sorts of traditions and it should come as no surprise that there are a fair number of damaging stories about church or synagogue. Pastors, priests, and rabbis, along with nuns, monks, and gurus, have done harm as well as good in the stories they have told their followers.

One story I have come across is of a young woman in Australia at the turn of the twentieth century. She has been brought up a strict Calvinist, so much so that for her the dogmas and stories of the harshest version of that form of

Christianity had the force of absolute truth. When she sat over a piece of needlework,

> she worked as if her life was in every stitch; as if one day the angel of the Last Judgment would hold up the pot-holder with its design of forget-me-nots, point to a stitch that was too small, or not straight, and say for the whole world, all the gathered souls of all the ages to hear: "Janet McIvor, did you do this?"[1]

It is not hard to figure out her "text." Captive to a story that told her only hard work and perfection would save her, she believed that even if she succeeded, she would never be sure.

Human beings cannot seem to get away from texts, whether they are the scriptures of the great religious traditions or the unwritten texts that we receive from our parents. "My mother always did it this way" or "My father always said," are appeals to texts that are as authoritative for some people as sacred writings. Sometimes rebellion is called for, but even rebellion presents problems; being in a perpetual state of revolt is another way of remaining under the spell of our past. People who plan their lives to be as *unlike* those of their parents as possible are as enslaved as those living under their thrall. Equally, there are biblical scholars whose whole life seems to be taken up in bashing fundamentalism as the revenge for their upbringing.

A more cheerful story comes from the cathedral in Lincoln, England. In the early seventeenth century the daughter of the dean was a devout Calvinist who was convinced that she was predestined for damnation. No amount of argument could dissuade her. One day, in the kitchen of the deanery, her father tried one more time to tell her that she was not damned. In a fit of anger she picked up a stone pitcher and threw it onto the stone floor.

"I am as surely damned as this pitcher will break!" The story goes that the pitcher did not break and she was so shocked that she cheered up, got married, had a large family, and lived into old age. Sometimes something can happen to us that disturbs and upsets the text of our lives—for good or ill.

No one can live entirely without an appeal to the authority of a story or text, and authority always has something to do with what we *think* is the truth. Sometimes rebellion and revolution are called for as accepted truths crumble and a new narrative emerges. Sometimes we have to get up and say, "You've got the story wrong. This is how it goes. Once upon a time...." In the case of the seventeenth-century clergyman's daughter, the pitcher did not break and a new story emerged.

❧ *Hidden Covenants*

A new story is possible when something happens to us to break the force of habit and recover our power to choose. We have a choice with regard to how we live in the world; each of us has a personal covenant with life and with God that is shaped by a story. These covenants and contracts stand at the center of our lives and go largely unexamined. They are rooted in our family of origin, in our desire to blame or be blamed, and in our longing to find causes and explanations for our discomfort and pain. We want our lives to be understandable and tidy, for "covenants which are unexamined or unexplored and underdeveloped are usually binding and inflexible."[2] They do harm to others and to ourselves.

One way to get at these hidden covenants is to ask, *"What is my unforgivable sin?"* What is it that causes you to spiral down, to freeze spiritually, to get stuck, to sit on your perch in the cage of your life when the door lies open before you?

Take Martha. She was the oldest in a large family. Her dad was strong, aloof, hard to please. Her way of pleasing was to be on top of things, hard-working, together. Her "unforgivable sin" was to appear weak, uncertain, lazy, incompetent. Her relationship with God? It was too deep and too hidden for her to acknowledge it, but it functioned something like this: "God will love me as long as I am competent, hardworking, together." Her ruling passion was to please and appease. Weakness, fear, and anger were not acceptable to God. Others found her difficult, driven, often judgmental. Hard on herself and others, "Pull yourself together!" was one of her favorite sayings.

Here is Simon's story. His dad was weak and ineffectual but still managed to be controlling—the tyranny of the weak over the strong. Simon, while not receiving much support for his accomplishments, did get support for his struggles, fears, and uncertainties. The unforgivable sin? To appear competent, strong, resourceful. His prayer to God? "I am your man as long as I give you the credit and as long as I am one of the meek and the weak." God was distant and overpowering. Deep down there boiled in Simon a resentment and anger at having to play the weakling. The price he paid was the suppression of a bright and quick mind.

What about Peter? His parents suppressed their feelings and his mother sent out pained signals threatening trouble if strong feelings were expressed. The sin? To hurt others by anger or aggression. Thus Peter's relationship with God was marked by caution and fear of messing up and being punished. His fear of hurting others made him come across as aloof and detached, and he often became angry without warning. When he did manage to bridge the terrible gap between himself and others, the consequences were often destructive. Peter was a genius at self-sabotage, and believing in a God who could strike him down at any second was no help.

Susan and Jim? They had a mother who insisted on being full of joy. Like Queen Victoria during the Boer War, who said, "There is no pessimism in this house and there will be none," she would not admit to any other emotion. The unforgivable sin was to be sad, because they knew that God required them to be happy—a belief that leads to excruciating patterns of emotional dishonesty. Secretly they came to hate their mother and her unrelentingly jolly God.

These hidden and not-so-hidden covenants we have with life and with God have the force of absolute truth. We feel that we have no choice because the covenant as received is, for us, *the* truth. Yet things can change: in that kitchen in seventeenth-century England the pitcher did not break, and a different and more generous version of life became available. The great enemy of freedom is fatalism—the acceptance of the inevitable as inevitable. Part of the work of truth is to subvert some of the texts we take for granted and reveal them as frauds. Even though *a* text is inevitable, it does not have to be *this* or *that* text. We have a choice.

Think of the way psychology tries to provide scientific explanations to explain our pains and conflicts. Chronic fatigue syndrome, Gulf War syndrome, sudden-wealth syndrome (it afflicts new young millionaires in Silicon Valley), stories of satanic ritual abuse and alien abductions —they are all *real*. The question is, to what reality do they refer? The problem lies not in the condition, which is real enough, but in the *naming* of it. By calling something a "syndrome," sufferers can give it the dignity of a strictly medical and physical origin. Scholar Elaine Showalter uses the word *hystery,* which is a story consciously or unconsciously designed to make unhappy lives interesting.[3] Does this sound harsh? It is. Showalter might be right in accusing us of struggling to make unhappy lives interesting, and she is surely right in claiming that many people have constructed a *hystery* for themselves that has the force of literal truth and enables them to live in the world. But is she prudent (let alone kind) to attack a person's system of inner validation?

Many of us are kept afloat by subscribing to an energizing lie, to the distortion of a particular text. To suggest that a person's treasured story about themselves could do with some revision is very threatening even when we sympathize with the condition. Even to suggest that sufferers from chronic fatigue syndrome might benefit from counseling and therapy is seen as undermining their basic text. The veterans of the Gulf War want to find a *physical* cause for their suffering. Are they merely deferring their reckoning with inner conflicts about the war and its aftermath? Could there be the revelation of deeper truth about their condition by simply admitting to the normal experiences of war—loneliness, fear, exhaustion, terror, guilt?

Often our *descriptions* of mental and spiritual states fit a particular cultural situation, and the descriptions change when times change. It isn't that we make up these things, but the way we choose to describe them changes. As a teenager, for example, I had to read a number of late-nineteenth-century poets for my French class at grammar school. All my adolescent experiences of emerging sexuality, falling in and out of love, and feelings of confusion, exhilaration, and shame were filtered through the work of these poets. I had a wonderful time wallowing in the romantic world of longing and self-hate, of ecstasy and transformation; this condition fitted with the world of my imagination. What was I, a seventeen-year-old, to do with experiences for which there was as yet no language? Puccini's opera *La Bohème* gave me a way of interpreting the chaotic mass of feelings inside me, and whenever I see and hear Puccini's opera all these old feelings return. But eventually I had to move on. Now, looking back, I realize that the text of my life has gone through many revisions, but I am not prepared to say that my seventeen-year-old self was wrong or mistaken. In fact, those nineteenth-century poets and Puccini's opera got me through a difficult period of transition by giving me images through which to recognize myself. They provided a makeshift map to help me move on.

Moving from one version of the text to another can, of course, be painful. When it comes to loneliness, fear, exhaustion, terror, and guilt, truth-telling can be excruciating and our resistance to it fierce. It is hard to decide which narratives need revision or need discarding. Which story should be our guiding light? The good news is that facts are stubborn things. We find ourselves drawn back to the place from which we started: respect for the facts, commitment to accuracy. A text is a particular interpretation of a set of facts, and it is good from time to time to review the facts we are interpreting.

✑ The Greatest Text

One of the great texts that millions have taken as their guiding light is the Bible. There is no settled agreement about its meaning and message, and battles between rival approaches are as alive today as ever. A great deal is at stake here because a revered text like the Bible has the power to hurt and to heal, depending on the community holding the key of interpretation. Some even believe that the Bible can interpret itself. The Bible is the truth and that's that! A flat, literalistic approach to the Bible-as-truth does damage both to the text and to those for whom it is the authority. In the past the Bible has been used to justify slavery and racism, the subjugation of women, and the wasting of the planet. It has been invoked to banish and alienate those who are different from the dominant group, such as gays and lesbians.

When I was growing up people still took literally St. Paul's injunction that women cover their heads in church.

After all, the divine rule came straight from the New Testament: "Ladies should wear hats in church!" It was a custom so entrenched that it had the force of an absolute truth. One of the great results in the pursuit of truth, however, is the unmasking of the ideas we take for granted. As we have seen, good scientists test their hypotheses over and over again. In fact, they try to disprove what they hope to be the case. It is a crucial element in our search for truth that we sometimes undermine the authority of concepts and constructs.

When it comes to the most influential text of our culture (either with regard to those who swallow the Bible whole or those who have reacted against it) there is no better guide than Old Testament scholar Walter Brueggemann. He writes that a revolution beginning in the late eighteenth century came to undermine old certainties that had been in place for well over a thousand years. The result, Brueggemann suggests, is that "atheism is now a credible, perhaps a consensus option for what is serious in life, and the articulation of life-with-God has become a risky intellectual outpost, perhaps as difficult and as odd and as embarrassing as was atheism in the seventeenth century."[4] In other words, who needs the God of the Bible? How could such an endlessly restless deity—who interfered in every human affair, including economics—be the object of rational belief?

But on closer examination the God of the Bible has a great deal to teach pilgrims of the truth, not least because much of it is written in Hebrew, a language well-suited to our journey since it is endlessly imprecise and unclear. Hebrew points to rather than explains, so that when we are looking for definitions and explanations we have to do damage to the text in order to find what we want—be it tax cuts, capital punishment, or a bloated defense budget. The Bible is an amazing vehicle for hints and suggestions, a game of hide-and-seek with the Divine, rather than a clear rule book. It is "filled with imprecision and inference and innuendo...contradiction, hyperbole, incongruity, disputation." Walter Brueggemann believes this way of thinking, feeling, and writing is important in a society like ours that prides itself on technological control and precision. He concludes that

> we are seduced into thinking that if we know the codes, we can pin all the meaning down, get all mysteries right and have our own way without surprise, without deception, without amazement, without gift, with miracle, without address, without absence, without anything that signals mystery or risk.[5]

In the pursuit of truth and the stories that seek to contain it, we need a way of speaking that opens and suggests and does not conclude or define.

The God of the Bible, according to Brueggemann, is a problem: irascible, elusive, and polyvalent, speaking with many voices. This God is capable of coming and going, judging and forgiving, speaking and remaining silent in ways that make the next time endlessly uncertain. This God drives Adam and Eve out of paradise, causes Abraham to wander off in old age into the wilderness to make a new beginning, allows his people to be enslaved in Egypt, and then leads them through a great deliverance into a promised land. This God gets angry and, like a wronged lover, grieves over betrayal. This God sends us his Son, who is executed and then vindicated in resurrection, calling his followers into a new life. In short, this God pushes us to the extremity of our imagination. The system is open, not closed. It is supple, not rigid. It is subject to revision.

An open, supple system is not wishy-washy but morally challenging. The God who looks out at us from the pages of the Bible contradicts the Nike version of reality that "life is for winners." The main text of our culture is that we are rivals of each other for finite and limited resources. As John Updike was once quoted in *The Wall Street Journal*, we may live "better" than most of the inhabitants of the planet but "the fact that compared to the inhabitants of Africa and Russia we still live well cannot ease the pain that we no longer live nobly." What might it mean to live nobly? To live in the knowledge that it is a holy and awesome thing to be human? What kind of story might draw us to such nobility?

Our dominant story of competitive violence tears at the social fabric by reducing life to a contest to see who can have the most and who can have it first. Author Michael Lewis, in his book about Silicon Valley and the new billionaires, *The New New Thing*, writes of a man who confesses that he is haunted by the dream of having more money than anyone else "just for one tiny moment."[6] What does this say about all of us? Can a narrative of trust be built on such values?

Truth is about trust, about a covenant that binds the haves and have-nots in one community. Truth in the end is about kinship. We are members one of another. We are pilgrims *to*, not possessors *of* truth. We have to be on the move and it is no accident that the second book of the Hebrew scriptures is called departure, *exodus*.

What is our story? Can we authorize an alternative story that contradicts our violent and isolating competitiveness? How rebellious are we prepared to become on behalf of the real? "The Real is what will strike you as really absurd," wrote W. H. Auden in his poem *For the Time Being*. If that is the case, then the journey will require great cunning. We will need to pay attention to many voices (including those rendered silent in the past) if we are to revise the texts wandering loose in our culture and make them more whole. Conversation will become an adventure, an encounter that not only changes the way we see the world but changes the world itself.

I want to be part of a conversation that offers me the possibility that I might come out of it a different person than I was when it began. Such a conversation requires a great deal of trust. I can never be sure of the outcome and I am not always willing to risk it. Better to score points, I say to myself, than be open to such an adventure. Our pursuit of truth requires a generosity borne of collaboration. Why put a positive and grateful construction on the world? Why not?

⌘ Biblical and Mystical Rebellion

The Hebrew Bible helps to make us rebellious, as does the Christian mystical tradition. For one thing, both the Bible and the mystics challenge us with the inexhaustibility of God. The tradition insists on a discipline that we would like to resist. In approaching the Hebrew scriptures, the rabbis followed the path of endless interpretation. No one has the last word. Theirs is an endless conversation about what the texts mean. The mystical life moves toward an end of which there is no end. Pilgrims share this vision of the universal and unending character of our journey to and in God. We want a guiding light to show us the way. The truth is that all things are lights (a stone, a piece of wood) but they are not the thing we seek.[7] The mystics believe that the universe is trying to tell us something about ourselves. What keeps our drive for facts from going haywire? The discovery of a higher form of knowing. It was St. Gregory the Great who coined the phrase: "Love itself is a form of knowledge."[8]

Mystics have a particular take on the Bible. They understand the continuities and discontinuities of *process* that are significant for our transformation, acknowledging that "*some* biblical texts could not be read literally and that *all* biblical texts were capable of many meanings."[9]

John Scottus Eriugena, the ninth-century Irish scholar, elucidated three principles of interpretation that speak to our contemporary situation:

∾ *Revelation in the Bible and creation must contain an infinite multiplicity of meanings.*

∾ *God is better known by not knowing.*

∾ *The distinction between fact and interpretation is of the utmost importance.*

Eriugena clearly favors "interpretation" over "facts." The point of reading the Bible is for mystical transformation, not for defending a particular position or punishing those whom we regard as deviant. At the end of the conclusion of his *Periphysion,* Eriugena generously states, "Let everyone hold to what opinion he will until that Light shall come that makes the light of the false philosophers a darkness and converts the darkness of those who truly know the light."[10]

The witness of the mystics is important because they not only see the world as a sacred place, they are also open to two texts *other* than the Bible: the Book of Nature and the Book of Experience. St. Bernard begins his analysis of the Song of Songs with these words: "Today let us read in the Book of Experience." These insights are preserved in the monastic tradition, which provides a model of community from which our fragmented society could learn a great deal. The shared life of a monastery meets the need of men and women for a moral compass, community formation, and food and shelter. Such a place would be ideal for the adventure of human conversation. Conversation is closer to conversion than we thought. We have to be in an *obedient* community, one where the members listen to each other. According to this tradition, life is the *peregrinatio pro Christo,* "exile for Christ's sake," an ongoing process of conversion. Conversion means continually being pierced to the heart, also called compunction—a form of clarity that makes us open to new possibilities. Like a good conversation, conversion offers the constant promise of change.

Let's end with three questions:

∾ *Which text most formed (or deformed) you as a person? What is your covenant?*

∾ *Who controls the story of your life? To whom have you surrendered the power to diagnose your condition?*

∾ *Which is the deeper truth: are we consumers or neighbors?*

Probing these questions will take a certain amount of cunning.

Chapter 6

Truth and Cunning

Surfaces can be seen, but depths must be interpreted.

There's an old saying: Truth *lies* in the interpretation. You need to say it to yourself a couple of times to get the double meaning. Truth requires interpretation and yet all interpretations are, to some extent, inaccurate or unreliable. Words mislead as well as reveal, lie as well as tell the truth. We can say even true things falsely. That is why telling the whole truth requires a special kind of cunning, because we do not always say what we mean or mean what we say.

Sometimes our actions say one thing and our words another. Years ago there was a cartoon on the front cover of the English magazine *Punch* that showed a cemetery in the center of which was a grave festooned with flowers. An elderly woman was kneeling by it, placing another bouquet on the grave and looking up at a friend. The caption read: "I come here everyday. He always hated flowers!" What *looked* like a loving act was, in fact, an act of spite. Without the caption, the picture would have expressed an entirely different emotion. Discerning the truth in a situation sometimes takes cunning.

At a dinner party not long ago, I found myself at a loss for words. This doesn't happen very often but on that particular occasion something in me froze. The subject was religion and the company sympathetic and congenial, but I suddenly realized something that has been true for some time: namely, that there is very little agreement on the meaning of the words we use to convey our deepest sensibilities. For example, if a certain kind of person asked me if I believed in God, I would be tempted to say "No!" simply because the word God in the mouth of many people is a code-word for prejudice, resentment, and repression. Martin Buber once wrote to the effect that even though the word "God" is, perhaps, the most abused word in the English or any language, we better hang onto it because something precious is lost when we try to do without it.

Another area of confusion is the sometimes cartoon-like world of morality. Moral discourse, such as it is, is often largely a matter of posturing and invocation, while the use of slogan and code-word is the order of the day. We have lost the skill of seeing our life as an art in which we try to discern many different levels of reality at work. The task of integrating them requires us to be able to live with their conflicts. Remember that each one of us is a work in progress, and it takes a long time to make a human being. Moral acts, it used to be said, are ones in which we express our true nature. Underneath all our moral struggles is the question, "What does it mean to be truly human?" Then we come back to the place where we started. What is the truth about John, about you, about me?

Like the actor Peter Brook describes, a human being is always struggling for form. I am much more sympathetic than I used to be of women and now men who spend a great deal of money on their hair and appearance, always struggling to preserve form in a situation that seems about to fall apart. The character Hans Castorp in Thomas

Mann's *The Magic Mountain* raises the question of these complex, interwoven levels in the mystery of being truly human. There is a sweet and painful precariousness about human efforts and projects. We are, he says, a "feverish, interwoven process of decay and repair" caught between matter and spirit, neither one nor the other, "like a rainbow above a waterfall."[1]

Being and staying alive is an art. It takes imagination and a sense of humor. There is also a word I have been skating around that has to do with flesh-taking-shape. The word is *incarnation*. Meaning has to have form. It is a principle of the spiritual life. When Christians talk about flesh and flesh-run-riot we cannot help but think of the God who creates us to be neighbors rather than consumers.

∾ *Practicing Trust*

As neighbors we need to recover the old humanizing disciplines of imagination, worship, and human conversation, which take a certain level of civility. The discipline of civility is liberating but I have great sympathy for those who have ceased to be civil. For one thing, the call to civility on the part of the powerful has always been a ploy to keep the powerless in their place. For another, civility requires that I treat my fellow citizens as people of good will. I'm not sure that I am up to such a risky act of trust. But the risk is essential if we are not to be continually at each other's throats. As Stephen Carter has pointed out, "Laws on sexual harassment and 'hate speech' sprout up when people do not share a code of civility."[2]

To be a person who feels and thinks deeply involves a commitment not only to practicing trust in an untrustworthy culture, but also to breaking the code of a corrupt language so that the truth may be spoken and lived. A tall order. To be someone committed to transformation and social justice means developing a kind of cunning, a sort of deviousness, so that the truth can be truly lived and told. But how can one be cunning and devious without undermining trust?

One way is for us to revive and respect the poetical imagination, which is both playful and profound. The age-old problem of confusing fact with truth never goes away. Truth and fact are different from each other yet intimately connected. As we have seen, we need research, scholarship, and honesty in sorting out facts from falsehoods, but we need the poetic imagination to tell the *whole* truth. It takes a poet to pay attention to the facts and then to tell the truth. We need ways of thinking, praying, and acting that are playful, cunning, *and* trustful. It takes imagination.

Trust and playfulness is also an antidote to the absurdities and cruelties of much of contemporary religion. Religion tends to be abused for political, ethnic, or personal advantage, so that "truth" becomes a weapon to do harm in the name of righteousness. At the same time, I am impressed with a new spirit at work within and between the great religious traditions. We may well be moving to a place where there is a critical mass of people who are committed to transformation and willing to explore what it might mean to expand the boundaries of our dreaming. I find myself on the move and do not hold beliefs in the same old way. We are in a time when basic definitions are being renegotiated: definitions of inclusion and exclusion, definitions of Christianity and of all the great religious traditions. It will take playfulness, trust, and cunning for us to get where we need to go.

How do we become less defensive so that we can discern that all is gift and enjoy the wealth of welcoming others into a more generous community? For one thing, we are discerning new forms of poverty, new forms of spiritual homelessness. Many of the new "homeless" are the affluent. The stunted imagination of many rich people is a source of their peculiar poverty, so it takes a peculiar form of compassionate cunning to get their attention. Their wealth protects them from the real world with the illusion that the world their riches have constructed is the only one that matters. Money is a vaccination again one of the most virulent diseases of the soul: boredom. "I'm bored. Let's go to Paris for the weekend." "I'm frightened. Let's buy another house." "I'm getting old. Let's kill time shopping." How do we storm these ramparts of privilege without creating a nightmare? Perhaps we might learn from God's method of slipping in among us unnoticed, in the form of a child. We might ponder the strangeness of God's cunning, who has to use odd methods to get our attention.

My own experience of God's cunning was shaped by a society ruled by class. God was so playful that the system was turned upside down. In spite of the hurt and silliness of class prejudice, I heard a gospel that proclaimed an aristocracy of being. We were all important in the eyes of God. We were all well-connected. We were all somebody. The vision of the gospel I received was romantic and inclusive even in the face of society's cruel divisions. I was taught that I am what my brothers and sisters are. If they are lost, then so am I. If they are found, then I am found, too.

I had to ask myself, What is the method by which the excluded can enter a group, change its structure, and give themselves a place at the table? One of my heroes in the Church of England was an Anglican monk, Herbert Kelly. After he failed in his effort to join the army (he had a hearing problem) and barely earned his degree at Oxford, he volunteered to train blue-collar Englishman for missionary work in Korea. The venture was a fiasco and Kelly was left with a group of trained men from the wrong side of the tracks. No one in Korea over a hundred years ago would have noticed that the men were not from the right class, but how would they get on if they were let loose in England? God's sense of humor prevailed and ordination was opened up to the working classes. God's cunning helps many cross such thresholds into a deeper truth.

∾ *The Cunning of the Liturgy*

The liturgy is one of the instruments of God's loving cunning. The sacrament of bread and wine unmasks us and feeds us at the same time. It undermines our view of things and inserts a joyful uneasiness about what we think is real and what we take for granted. The liturgy is designed to enchant, to disenchant, and to reenchant all at the same time. Part of the church's task today is to be subversive, but subversion must be driven by gratitude and joy, not resentment and fear. The point is not to terrify us into change but to open us up to who we really are—children of God, sisters and brothers to each other. None of us is dispensable, "good for nothing."

Mozart's *Coronation* Mass is the exultation of Mary, a Jewish peasant girl, as the Queen of Heaven. From one point of view this is daft, but Christians celebrate a God whose grammar involved the revolution of language, of definitions. The rich are sent away empty. God's new language tells us that we have mistaken the true nature of power. The name of the game is freedom—slipping the trap of received wisdom. Weaving a new world in place of the old.

Think for a moment of what was once considered a secure world backed by a clear national story. Stephen Carter's *Civility: Manners, Morals, and the Etiquette of Democracy* describes the apparently solid world of America in the early sixties. It was the world of Ed Sullivan, the automobile, the Pledge of Allegiance, and the two-party system. They all spoke of *certainty*. In the late fifties and early sixties America still saw itself as special in the eyes of God, undefeated in war and going through a remarkable industrial expansion. Carter writes,

Part of this celebration of America was the deep belief that the nation could never place its moral foot wrong—not for more than a short time. Racial segregation was accepted because it was the way America had always done business. There was one unique American race, and then there were other people, living here almost by accident, not yet entitled to all the benefits the nation offered to white people.[3]

Novelist Maxine Hong Kingston echoes these thoughts when she writes of the experience of Chinese immigrants. When she went to kindergarten and had to speak English for the first time, she became silent and so quiet that she flunked kindergarten. Language (or the lack of it) and shame go together. Say your parents come from China, Mexico, Poland, or Tibet. What happens when people can detect "the old country" in the way you speak? What about those strange-smelling spices you put in your food? And those stories you bring with you from another place? Where do they fit in? Wouldn't it be safer to remain silent?

Children who live in two worlds are vulnerable to several shames, several sets of eyes watching them. Most obviously, of course, both the parents and the school want the child to know that their way is *the* way, and that other ways lack true dignity. Immigrant children get to be shamed, first *by* their parents, and then they get to be ashamed *of* their parents."[4]

It is all very well if you are in the in-group, but what if you are an outsider? Or what if you find yourself on the inside, but with a heap of people above you who think that they are your "betters"? What happens when you refuse to "know your place"? What if a truth inside you burning to be told has been relegated to the margins and told to keep quiet?

The story of Frederick Douglass is of a subversive who stole his life back from those who had taken it from him. Born in 1818 in Talbot County, Maryland, his master Aaron Anthony was the overseer on the plantation of Colonel Edward Lloyd. Then Douglass became a house slave in Baltimore in the home of his master's in-laws, Hugh and Sophia Auld. Sophia did the unforgivable: she taught the eight-year-old how to read. By doing so, she showed that she did not know the "truth" of slavery; she did not know how to treat a slave. In this simple, cunning act in the service of truth, Sophia undermined the received world of her time. She "did not deem it impudent...for a slave to look her in the face."[5]

Douglass later said that once he began learning to read, he "understood the pathway from slavery to freedom." He wrote in his autobiography,

> All the education I possess, I may say, I have stolen as a slave. I did manage to steal a little knowledge of literature, but I am now in the eyes of the American law a thief and a robber, since I have not only stolen a little knowledge of literature, but have stolen my body also.[6]

Escaping from slavery in 1838, Douglass settled in New Bedford, Massachusetts, and became active in abolitionist circles. Was he right to learn to read and free himself? From our perspective the question is absurd, even grotesque. But imagine how it looked in 1838. After all, according to law, he *belonged* to Colonel Lloyd. How could this be *true*? The world that most people took as the *true* world thought that owning another human being was normal and acceptable. When you are in a world that you experience as a great lie, how do you change the "false truth" into a liberating one?

What do you do when you are born into a world where two distinct moral systems are in conflict? Some of us have to move between these worlds as freed slaves, as Douglass freed himself out of slavery and stole the most precious gift of all, literacy. One of our tasks is to steal the restored image of God back from those who diminish others. What rules, for example, should we violate in obedience to the inclusive and subversive table of the eucharist?

∾ *The Cunning Work of Truth*

Truth-tellers are called to disturb boundaries, erase thresholds, and muddy clear divisions, because—to use the language of faith—in Christ there is a new creation. We do our subversive work in story and song, two classic ways in which the social order is maintained and challenged at the same time.

Frederick Douglass acquired a white voice! How dare he? He even had the gall to rename himself several times. At birth he was Frederick Augustus Washington Bailey; then, when he moved north, he became Frederick Dailey, then Frederick Stanley, Frederick Johnson, and finally Frederick Douglass, after the hero in Walter Scott's *Lady of the Lake*. How about that as a journey of redefinition? He hoped for a community that did not shape itself in terms of color, but his hopes were dashed. The white churches in New Bedford made him sit in a separate pew, and he was subjected to the racism of the abolitionists, who treated him as a specimen of their cause. Beneath the experience of Frederick Douglass lies the maxim coined by Simone Weil, who called contradiction "a lever of transcendence." Contradiction helps us identify false truths and move into more generous ones. It becomes a means of transformation. Truth-tellers are always looking to change the rules of engagement that diminish and enslave us.

The task is to find a way of being in the world that is *both* public and hidden, and to find our role without being insincere. How do we develop the diplomatic skills necessary to serve the cause of humanity without having our heads chopped off? The process of integration requires cunning, the old principle of losing oneself to find oneself. We become authentically human by transcending ourselves, by being pushed beyond what we think are our limits.

The danger is that we can find ourselves enslaved by a half-truth at the expense of the whole. In *The Name of the Rose,* the medieval detective William of Baskerville tells his student, Adso, "The Antichrist can be born from piety itself, from excessive love of God or of the truth."

> Perhaps the mission of those who love mankind is to make people laugh at the truth, *to make truth laugh,* because the only truth lies in learning to free ourselves from the insane passion for the truth.[7]

The biographer of the artist Marcel Duchamp tells this story about the artist's death. Almost every evening before retiring Madame Duchamp and her husband were in the habit of reading funny stories aloud to each other. The joke would leave them both laughing just before going to bed. Late in the evening of October 1, 1968, it was his turn to read and, as usual, when the punch line came, they both laughed exuberantly. But on this particular evening, after laughing, Duchamp went to the bathroom and died. His wife went to look for him and found him lying on the floor, fully dressed. She said, "Much as I miss him, I am so grateful for the almost magic way he died."[8]

What a way to die! And what a way to live. What an incentive to wake up and live each day as a gift. There is a special happiness in "letting the world happen." The art is to allow the world to offer itself to us every day for our imagination, and to hesitate—just for a moment—before we start interpreting it. Wonder eludes us when we insist on having a "fix" on everything. When we come to the

world without an agenda, something magical happens—
real presence. That's why the sacramental is primary. The
radiance and clarity of presence is momentary but real,
while God is more generous and more complex than we
can ever imagine, pushing us always into a larger world
with larger sympathies. I hope to die laughing, caught by
God's cunning.

～

part three

Truth as Relationship

∾

Chapter 7

Pilgrims of the Truth

We are pilgrims of the truth; we haven't arrived.

As we get older, the full truth about ourselves involves a long story of mistakes, betrayals, loves, failures, and successes. That is what it means to pass through time. We change and the past cannot be undone. When we look back over our lives there is more and more to regret. (There is much to be thankful for, too, but it is often the failures that stick in our minds.) Perhaps we did something despicable in 1978, something we are still ashamed of in 1984, something that can't be undone in 1999. All these events are "true." How can they be woven into a truer story of hope? Our longing for truth becomes much more like a longing for integrity and forgiveness than the longing to rearrange the facts of the past in our favor. Truth becomes a matter of relationship, and the great biblical word for it is *covenant*.

As we get older, truth is increasingly embedded in the unfolding story of the mistakes, betrayals, loves, and failures that make up our lives. We also discover other stories—large, glorious, and terrible—that deepen our understanding of what it is to be a human being. There are myths and allegories giving us clues about our relationship to the world, to others, and to our deepest selves. Truth becomes a matter of trust and is found in the threads of a narrative. Even more important, our relationship to the truth becomes more and more like a relationship to a person, a matter of falling in love, with all the ups and downs of a love affair.

One of the great stories of the soul struggling for and with truth is John Bunyan's *Pilgrim's Progress*. The hero has to leave his home and make a long journey to find his true self in the Celestial City. Bunyan's famous hymn is familiar even to many who have never read his book.

> He who would valiant be
> 'gainst all disaster,
> let him in constancy
> follow the Master.
> There's no discouragement
> shall make him once relent
> his first avowed intent
> to be a pilgrim.

The hymn goes on to tell of the struggle the pilgrim has with the narratives about himself and the world that would bring him down. Bunyan describes his inner battle as one with lions, giants, hobgoblins, and foul-fiends—all symbols for those energies in his soul that would tempt him to despair and self-hate. When I reread *Pilgrim's Progress* I asked myself, "Was Bunyan mad?" His Puritan mid-seventeenth-century world is far from my own, but I discovered that he was onto something profoundly true about human experience that transcended his own time.

John Bunyan was born in 1628 and grew up in that stormy period leading to the English Civil War, the beheading of Charles I in 1649, and the establishment of Oliver Cromwell's rule. Charles II's restoration to the throne in 1660 was followed by a violent reaction against those who had followed and supported Oliver Cromwell. Among them was Bunyan, who was imprisoned as a dissenter for twelve years and upon his release became pastor of a separatist church in Bedford. He died in 1688 just as the period of religious persecution was ending. Today Puritanism is much maligned, caricatured as merely a restrictive list of moral prohibitions and a religion driven by sexual guilt, but in its time Puritanism was a fiery religious and social movement. Bunyan lived and wrote as part of a cultural revolution.

The full title of Bunyan's allegory, published in 1678, helps us understand his inner journey: *The Pilgrim's Progress from This World To That Which is to Come: Delivered under the Similitude of a Dream Wherein is Discovered the Manner of his Setting Out, his Dangerous Journey, and Safe Arrival at the Desired Country.* He wrote the first part in prison as a Baptist preacher, which begins: "As I walked through the wilderness of this world, I lighted on a certain place to sleep: and as I slept I dreamed a dream." He dreams of a man called Christian, who is clothed in rags, with the Bible in his hand and a great burden on his back. The burning question of the allegory is, "What shall I do to be saved?"

The first person Christian meets on his journey toward the Celestial City is a man named Evangelist, who directs him to the Wicket Gate—the narrow gate of the New Testament—where he will be told what to do. There follows a series of adventures, pitfalls, and temptations until Christian reaches the gate where a character called Good Will sends him on his way to the Celestial City. Yet his journey has barely begun. Christian has to move through a whole range of experiences of doubt, despair, error, and ignorance. He has still to negotiate the seductions of the world (Vanity Fair) and listen to the arguments of false friends. In the end Christian reaches the gate of the Celestial City:

I see myself now at the end of my journey, my toil-
some days are ended. I am going now to see that
head that was crowned with thorns, and that face
that was spit upon, for me. I have formerly lived by
hear-say and faith, but now I go to where I shall live
by sight, and shall be with him, in whose company
I delight myself.[1]

What a journey—packed with a cast of characters
from Bunyan's inner world! There is Mr. Worldly
Wiseman who, with pompous self-assurance, tries to con-
vince Christian that he would be better off simply to be
nominally and respectably religious. Why not take up res-
idence in the village of Morality under the care of Legality
and his son Civility?

Provision is there also cheap and good, and that
which will make thy life more happy, to be there
thou shalt live by honest neighbors, in credit and
good fashion.

Bunyan also introduces us to Mr. No-good, Mr.
Malice, Mr. Live-loose, Mr. High-mind, and Mr. Hate-
light. There are also characters named Formality,
Hypocrisy, and Talkative. Yet all the people Christian
meets on the road are looking for some lost glory, even
Obstinate, Pliable, Mistrust, Timorous, Turn-away, and
old Atheist. We all encounter characters like these in one
form or another on our spiritual journey, although perhaps with other names.

One of the most important characters Christian meets
is Valiant-for-Truth, who tells us that truth cannot be
taken for granted. We have to fight for it, stand up and
take sides. Truth is not easily won nor easily defended. It
calls us out of our comfortable existence to go on pilgrimage. The way to the Celestial City is full of danger, and the
pilgrim will encounter the Slough of Despond, the Hill of

Difficulty, and the Valley of Humiliation. "They told me also," Bunyan writes,

> of Giant Despair, of Doubting Castle, and of the ruins that the pilgrims met with there. Further, they said I must go over the Enchanted Ground, which was dangerous. And that after all this I should find a River over which I should find no bridge, and that the River did lie betwixt me and the Celestial Country.

To be committed to the truth is to be betrothed to it. And like all intimate relationships, it is subject to betrayal and disappointment, forgiveness and reconciliation.

∾ *A Spiritual Awakening*

I was drawn to reread Bunyan's great classic because, morally speaking, he was a man who had come to the end of his rope. Deeper truth—the wisdom for which the soul longs—emerges when we come to the end of our rope, when we have nothing left with which to negotiate. We hope that a version of the story of our lives will emerge that will portray us in a good light; we want the truth about ourselves to be self-justifying. What happens when things do not turn out right even after all our strategies of manipulation and self-deception? In the end we are left with the bits and pieces of a life that cry out for healing, for some good news. This, at least, was Bunyan's experience. He found that there was no way for him to be "righteous" on his own. Truth, whatever it was, brought the whole of who he was into the life of faith, including the things that are often suppressed: instinct, passion, and desire. Bunyan took every level of his experience seriously and forged it not only into a Christian allegory but also into a universal myth that any openhearted person might painfully and joyfully read. I love and admire Bunyan's allegory because he helps me recover my life as a moral adventure without falling into either moralism (self-justification) or despair (self-hatred).

I also value the book's emotional honesty and range of feelings and passions. Bunyan writes of rebellion and pride, resignation and resentment, as well as faith, hope, and love. Above all there is invitation—the embracing of truth and its disciplines as a way of freedom for the sake of a deepening sense of relationship with the world, with others, and with ourselves.

Pilgrim's Progress follows the classic threefold pattern of spiritual awakening. The Puritan psychology of conversion has much to teach us about the pilgrimage to and with truth. We begin with conviction of sin, which is first and foremost the process of awakening the soul so that the pilgrimage may begin. The pilgrim, however, soon moves into the second phase, which is falling flat on one's face in the futile attempt to build a spiritual life on religious practices and acts of moral righteousness. Then comes the third phase: the gradual education of the convert by means of the saving stories of scripture, which is a way of feeding the life of the imagination and providing a framework by which we can interpret our struggles, temptations, and joys.

Another way of looking at these three phases is to see the first as an encounter with a terrifying emptiness that we naturally resist but cannot defeat. Only then does grace emerge as that which sustains and loves us. The philosopher A. N. Whitehead suggested that we must first encounter Truth/God as void and as enemy before we can encounter the Divine as friend. Paula Reeves, a Jungian psychotherapist, identifies these three responses as defiance, compliance, and invitation. All three are important at various stages of our lives, but it would be a poor kind of life that found itself stuck in either defiance or compliance and never experienced life as invitation—as sheer gift and delight, a glimpse of the Celestial City.

I find echoes of these stages in my own experience and in that of others, such as the great psychoanalyst Carl Jung, who tells us that, after he was well-established in his profession, he still had to climb down and down into his own heart and accept the little clod of earth that he was. I think of the novelist John Updike's unlikely hero in *Rabbit Run,* who says, "There is something out there that wants me to find it."[2] This was Bunyan's intuition, too. The scientist Freeman Dyson puts it another way: "The universe knew we were coming."[3] We are meant to be here. The pursuit of truth becomes a pilgrimage in which truth pursues us. Truth attracts, lures, desires us. For the pilgrim truth is the *mysterium tremendum et fascinans,* the mighty and alluring mystery of the mystics.

Bunyan's story also teaches me to approach the mystery not as an intellectual puzzle to be solved, but as something to be lived. I am often asked by people seeking faith, "May I come to church even if I can't believe all that we say and do?" Pilgrims have to start where they are, just as Bunyan did, at the end of his rope and, in his particular case, in a prison cell. Each of us soon discovers something of the art of suffering, death, and transformation. They become a doorway into our own mystery.

Bunyan's universal myth took every level of his experience seriously—including his instincts and basic drives—and turned them into characters in a story. The truth of which he was a pilgrim challenged him to be available to transformation. What is the myth that holds the modern imagination captive? Is it the human being as prisoner or the human being as pilgrim? Bunyan's allegory (and behind Bunyan are the great stories of the Bible) teaches us the relationship between truth and narrative. Facts are not enough. We need a story that is full and detailed enough to be faithful to the facts. But what is the point of the story? The story is for the building of a community of trust and freedom. This is why it is important to tell the truth and live it. Without it, nothing hangs together. There can be no community, no communion.

I long to know who I am. To find out, I must go on pilgrimage. In the quest for truth, we are as much those who are probed as those who do the probing. Truth-telling has something to do with how all the bits and pieces of experience fit together in a truthful story. For people of faith, truth is deeply personal. It has to be. In fact, truth is a *person* and our truth is uncovered only in relationship with the divine truth who loves and sustains us.

The truth comes to us in the form of a story that provides a way for us to interpret our experience. But it isn't *just* a story. The narrative becomes not only an interpreter of experience but the medium of experience, too. Through it we experience ourselves as known, loved, and accepted because the truth loves us and is willing to suffer for us. *Crux probat omnia* is a gospel principle: "the cross tests everything." It is one of the benchmarks of truth, like the image of a mother with her baby and an invitation to the banqueting table. These images locate me in a love story and tell me who I am.

A young officer in the First World War was in charge of looking after a young man who had been severely wounded in combat. Not only was he gassed and shell-shocked, he was also blinded and his memory was gone. The other men in the unit enjoyed boxing as recreation, and one day the young officer took the wounded man into the ring and asked that if any one recognized him, would they please shout out? No one said a word. Silence. The man screamed, "Can nobody tell me who I am?" In telling this story, Eric James comments:

> We all want to discover who we are, but that so often means an anxious struggle for survival as a person among persons, on the part of basically unloved and injured individuals, who have never

been able to feel sure of ourselves, and who are haunted by feelings of timidity, unworthiness, inferiority, shyness and loneliness.[4]

I imagine Bunyan felt that way in his prison cell—cold, abandoned, fearful, wondering who he was and dreaming his great dream.

∾ *The Truth About You, About Me?*

Imagine. It is early one morning. I am sitting in my study wondering how I came to be the way I am—sixty years old, divorced after thirty years, now remarried, a priest in the Anglican Communion. Mine is hardly a success story, yet in spite of the ups and downs of my life, with its share of shame, sorrow, and regret, I have never been happier or felt better. I wonder, what is the truth about my life? Who would I trust to tell it? Our lives have many interpreters besides ourselves: our parents, our friends, our enemies, those who maximize and those who minimize our gifts and our faults.

A letter written at the time of Princess Diana's death by the former dean of an English cathedral said, "Only the young die good. We live by myths and fairy tales. What if Romeo in middle age becomes lecherous and corpulent and Juliet irritable and prone to migraines? I look in my mirror and see this raddled old cynic, duplicitous, hypocritical and selfish. And once I was a beautiful young priest. I could have been so remembered if I had died at thirty-nine."[5] Only the young die good? That is why I returned to Bunyan's *Pilgrim's Progress* at a time of deep transition in my life. I had come to the end of my rope and deep questions of faith were being raised in new ways. I wondered how I might interpret my life truthfully, without self-deception on the one hand and despair on the other. Who or what, I wondered, has the last word about us?

How have you tended to tell the story of your life? As if it were not yours but someone else's? Someone you don't know well? Someone who isn't either interesting or important? How have others told it? Do you see yourself as the victim of other people's distortions or as a character in a story in which you are desired and desirable? Are you a slave or a pilgrim? Are you an isolated individual or is every living thing a neighbor? What you think of as true will depend on your answer.

How far, I wonder, do I sum up the truth of my times? Each one of us, in a sense, is the summation of vast depths of human experience. We are all unique and yet the recipients of what our parents and the world passed onto us in the way of *received* truths. I was taught both wonder and distrust as a child. "The world is not to be trusted!" "Happiness is an illusion, so grab what you can while you can!" These were articles of belief.

What we think of as true often depends on what we believe the world is like. As author Sam Keen says, *the poverty or richness of our loving determines our sense of what is real.* Love is the key because love is the highest form of knowledge. We know the power of falling in love. This basic human experience reconstitutes the world for the lovers just as falling out of love destroys the inner worlds that were once so real. Truth-telling is a matter of imaginative storytelling that does justice to the wide range of human experience beginning with Bunyan's moment of truth—our coming to the end of our rope.

Terry Waite, the former emissary of the Archbishop of Canterbury, is an example of a modern pilgrim who relied on his memory and imagination to pull him through the terrible experience of being held hostage in Beirut for 1763 days, many of them in solitary confinement. His method of survival? He had nothing with which to write, so he composed in his imagination. He set about reviving his memories and rehearsing his life, reconstructing his life as a narrative. Sometimes it was too stressful and often he feared for his life and his mental stability, but the *story* sustained him: "I always managed to return to my story and thus was enabled to preserve my sanity and identity."[6] How willing are we to train our perception and nourish our impoverished imaginations by reading such saving stories as Bunyan's *Pilgrim's Progress?*

❧ *The Story of the Three Warnings*

Once there was a shopkeeper in Italy, with a wife and three sons, who on the morning of his thirtieth birthday found a corpse on the doorstep. He was horrified. Perhaps he would be accused of murder? So he panicked and ran away, settling down in a city miles away from his home and family. There he was given a job by the wisest of men whose name (of course) was Solomon. Hundreds of people came from far and wide to ask Solomon's advice and they paid handsomely for it.

Our hero worked hard and saved up his wages. Deep down in his heart he dreamed of returning to his family one day. Like the rest of us, he had signed up with someone (or something) that he thought would look after him and give him immunity, but eventually he became restless and dissatisfied. Finally he could bear it no longer and decided to head for home. After all, he had been working hard for twenty years and had saved up all of three hundred crowns, a tidy sum.

Solomon was sorry to see him go and offered him some advice before he set out on his homeward journey. He knew that advice from Solomon didn't come cheap but reluctantly he agreed to three pieces of advice for the usual fee of one hundred crowns apiece. He knew he'd been had when he heard the first piece of advice: *"Don't leave the old road for a new one. Go back the way you came!"*

"I gave you one hundred crowns for that?!"

"Yes! It will help you remember!"

The second piece of advice seemed as useless as the first: *"Don't meddle in other people's affairs."* As for the third, it drove him to distraction: *"Save your anger until the following day!"* He felt he'd been conned. To make matters worse, Solomon not only took his three hundred crowns but gave him a cake in a heavy box to share with his family! "I worked twenty years for this," he muttered as he lugged the box and his few belongings along with him, leaving as poor as when he arrived.

Not long after leaving Solomon's house, he met a band of young and happy travelers. They suggested a detour to a tavern up in the mountains. Our hero was ready to go with them when he remembered Solomon's first piece of expensive advice: *"Don't leave the old road for a new one. Go back the way you came!"* Half an hour later he heard gunshots and screams. The young group had been ambushed and our man was grateful that he remembered Solomon's simple words.

What can such pedestrian advice mean for us? Surely it doesn't mean we should close ourselves off from new experiences? Perhaps it is telling us that we already have all the experience we need to know what kind of life to choose. Perhaps it is an invitation to get to know ourselves over again.

Meanwhile, back in the story, it was getting dark and our hero found himself in a forest in front of a mean and unwelcoming cottage. What was he to do? It was late and he was hungry. He knocked on the door and a large brute of a man grudgingly agreed to give him supper in exchange for his doing a few chores in the morning. As they were eating their simple and unattractive meal of dry bread and thin soup, there was a knocking under the floorboards and the host lumbered to a trap door and opened it. From the basement there came a pathetic, ragged creature, blind and wild with hunger yet submissive to the large man, who took a skull from the sideboard and filled it with soup. She ate it hurriedly and noisily and was then sent back to her prison. "What do you think of that?" asked the brute of a man as soon as the trapdoor was fastened shut. Just as our hero was about to give his grim host a piece of his mind, he remembered the second piece of advice: *"Don't meddle in other people's affairs."* Instead of tearing into his host for his cruelty, he answered, "You must have a good reason."

"I do. You're the first guest to have survived my hospitality. Others who have disagreed with me have had their throats cut. That woman is my wife. Years ago she took a lover behind my back. That skull was his."

Let's stop the story for a moment and ask ourselves what is going on here. Is our hero a prudent coward, out to save his own skin? Or is the story about something deeper and more disturbing? Has our traveler met part of himself locked in that cellar? What can a heartless man in a hovel with a broken woman in the basement tell us about ourselves and our world? We meet people like that every day wounded, resentful, with every excuse for their behavior. They have condemned part of their existence to the cellar and they will not forgive it for hurting them. We catch a glimpse of it when we hear the hint of self-righteousness in our voice. We have to face the truth we have hidden from the world.

Back to the story. Now our hero was almost home. It was getting dark but there was joy in his heart as he made his way to his old village. As he approached the house, he could hear music and laughter. In the well-lit window of his former home he saw his beautiful wife, but to his horror she was dancing with a handsome young man. They were obviously the center of a great celebration. Angry, he reached for his dagger. "I'll kill them both!" Just as he was about the burst into the room he remembered Solomon's third piece of costly advice. *"Save your anger until the following day!"* He slipped his knife into its sheath and sullenly walked out of the village to spend the night in the woods. At dawn, still bent on murder, he met an old neighbor and friend on the street. "You're back! You should have been here last night. Your oldest son is about to be ordained a priest and last night there was a great party to send him on his way! There was music and dancing!" Our hero was stunned. He had come close to murdering his wife and son. He hurried home and threw his arms around his joyful if surprised wife. After a great deal of hugging and kissing all round, he remembered the heavy cake Solomon had given him in its box. Inside the cake, he found three hundred crowns![7]

The point of this story is easy to see, but it is hard to decide on any one meaning. In fact, there is a disturbing openness about it that makes endless interpretation possible. A good story initiates a conversation where no one has the last word. "Stick to the path!" How dull and pedestrian! "Mind your own business!" How self-centered and timid! "Save your anger until the morning!" How calculating and cold-blooded! But the story invites us to take a second look. We do not even have to accept or believe the great stories and allegories about human longing and fulfillment for them to be useful. Sometimes there is a head-on collision between us and a story, and the result is a reshaping of the material to add to the great library of human experience.

I told this story once to a group of students, and one stayed up all night because the story made her angry. She rewrote the part about the woman in the basement, and in this new version the woman was rescued from her underground prison. This was a fruitful and important exercise for the student, and her version of the story deepened all of our experience. We became a more whole and trusting *community* because we were capable of accepting the story as written *and* rebelling against it at the same time. The story elicited multiple interpretations as we became involved in conversation with each other. The story pushed us deeper into communion, into community.

As we journey with and toward truth, our apprehension of it becomes more and more a matter of trust, of betrothing, like two lovers committing themselves to each other. Truth is what makes us and holds us in being, what heals and restores, what probes, tests, and comforts us on our journey, what desires us and fulfills all our longing. We are all pilgrims with and toward the truth.

~

Chapter 8

Truth as Betrothal

We are betrothed to one another. The world is a wedding.

The poet R. P. Blackmur writes of language, "Words verge on flesh and so we may/ Someday be to ourselves the things we say." One day I would like to experience fully this inner integrity of which the poet speaks. I would like to *be* the things I say, and become the meeting place of love and knowledge. I would like to be at home with the sacred. I would like to be true. The Christian mystical tradition bears witness to this longing for the kind of knowing that integrates, bringing together thought, feeling, and experience. Knowledge and love come together in God in a way of knowing that is unlike "scientific" ways of knowing. This other way of knowing is a kind of communion, calling for a radical openness of spirit. This is why one of our tasks is to examine the ways in which we close ourselves off from life and love.

One ancient way of talking about sin was to describe the sinner as *curvatus in se,* "curved in on oneself." When I am curved in on myself I become a lie. If I want to be true, I have to unbend and open up. When I tell a lie I then become captive to it. If I don't want to be owned by others, I must struggle to be a truth-teller. Otherwise

> the people you have to lie to, own you. The things
> you have to lie about, own you. When your children see you owned, then they are not your children
> anymore, they are the children of what owns you. If
> money owns you, they are the children of money. If
> your need for pretense and illusion owns you, they
> are the children of pretense and illusion. If your fear
> of loneliness owns you, they are the children of
> loneliness. If your fear of the truth owns you, they
> are the children of the fear of truth.[1]

The truth for which I long is a covenanted truth, one by which I am held and known. Truth invites me into a partnership that is a form of betrothal. I want to be *wedded* to the truth. In what the Christian mystical tradition calls *Brautmystik,* "Bride-mysticism," God is our lover, companion, and friend calling us into relationship, into covenant. Our relationship with the truth, therefore, is like falling in love. When we fall in love, we disappoint and hurt each other; we say we are sorry and are forgiven.

✹ Truth and Betrothal

Truth is betrothing, plighting our troth, promising our truth to one another. Our desire for God is stirred up in our longing for each other, as the poet John Donne wrote about his wife Ann: "Here the admiring her my mind did whet, to seek thee, God." We awaken in each other the desire for God and get into a fine old mess because we become confused and try to turn the person we love into a god responsible for our happiness. No human being can bear the burden of divinity. That is why lovers often hurt and disappoint each other.

Most of us are aware of a spirituality of yearning desire, of yielding to the unknown. The Spirit is the divine reaching out beyond itself to create us. Christ is the bride-groom of the soul. The actor Alec Guinness speaks of running through the streets of London simply to sit before the Blessed Sacrament as if running to be with a lover. Imagine that! To sit with the truth as with a lover.

So, when we talk about God we are talking about covenant and communion. We are talking about trust. That is why, before anyone mentions the word "God," I want to know if the speaker can be trusted. God speaks to us in the stories of the Bible and in the banquet of the liturgy as One who calls us to be not only companions but also sharers of the divine. The ancient rabbis spoke of the Torah (the first five books of the Hebrew Bible) as a beautiful princess locked in a tower. She has to be wooed, courted, and loved.

What about religious institutions? How can we learn to trust them? Some years ago I read a book called *The Man with the Power* by Leslie Thomas. It is about a crazy group of itinerant and disreputable evangelists traveling on two buses, on their way to Las Vegas. "One day," he writes,

> we would be happy and hopefully traveling, and the next sullen with failure and boredom. We were to find interest, even joy, love perhaps, and always surprise, among our good companions, and in the next hour flames of anger, frustration, dislike and even disgust. It would be strangers on an up-and-down emotional ride, tied together for better or, frequently, for worse.... There were times when those of us who believed and those who did not believe were closely one. It was the same journey for us all.

This strikes me as an apt description of the church. "The same journey for us all." The truth is that we are all betrothed to each other. The world is a wedding! I wake up to the truth that my life is not my own. I am who I am because there is Another who holds me in being.

St. Augustine wrote of the *cor inquietum*, "the restless heart." The heart is a movement toward the divine and can only come to rest in God: "You have made us for yourself and our hearts are restless until they rest in you." Our life is a betrothal, a vision and promise of cooperative delight. Truth-as-betrothal demands that we cherish the flesh, the material, the five senses, as the means by which love is embodied and expressed. Incarnation.

The conviction that truth is a betrothal came to me when my own body demanded attention because of the problems most men of my age face. I followed the body's lead, ate more healthily, took more exercise, lost weight, and, in general, felt more at home in the world and in the body. But this discovery was more than exercise. It was a radical appreciation of incarnation, of not only *having* a body but *being* a body. Toni Morrison powerfully express-es something of what I mean in her novel *Beloved*, when she writes, "*You* got to love it. *You*!...This is flesh I'm talking about here. Flesh that needs to be loved."[2]

Seeing the world as the theater of betrothal leads us into other ways of knowing. The question of epistemology (how can we know anything?) in the life of faith is not so much what can I know, but who can I trust? This need to be able to trust becomes intensely focused when we are chronically ill or dying. Do you want your physician to be absolutely truthful when it comes to your medical condi-tion? Years ago the medical profession hid behind a mys-tique of "expertise," and physicians weren't expected to disclose information that they thought wasn't immediate-ly relevant to the treatment in hand. Nowadays we expect more. Many of us want the whole picture. I want a doctor who tells the truth, a doctor I can trust. When I am dying, I don't want to be pushed out of life prematurely, nor do

I want to be forced to stay when it's time to go. I need a community of trust in which to do my living and dying.

Take Michael. He is twenty-six and last year experienced weakness in his arm and, although he had no headache, his eyes kept blurring. The symptoms went away in about twelve hours. His doctor sent him to a neurologist for the usual round of tests. Michael was told not to worry about the episode and thought no more about it. In fact, he's had no episodes since. But the letter sent to his physician by the neurologist states that Michael almost certainly has multiple sclerosis. Further, in the letter the neurologist states that in order to prevent excessive worry he does not, as a matter of course, inform patients in the early stages of multiple sclerosis of their diagnosis.

What would you do if you were the neurologist? What would you want if you were Michael? How is Michael best respected as a person? Doctors, understandably, are hesitant to share uncertainty with their patients (or, as we say now, consumers). In 1961, ninety percent of a sample of physicians in the United States said that they would not disclose a diagnosis of cancer to a patient; less than twenty years later, ninety-seven percent said they would.[3] The desired relationship we would have with our physician is surely rather like a betrothal.

What breaks the covenant between us? Sometimes it is the arrogant conviction that we know the whole truth. Many of us are tempted to "tell it like it is." It is even easier when we are angry at someone, so that truth-telling becomes a weapon to assert power over another. My antennae go up when someone says, "I'm just being honest," for usually it is a prelude to saying something hurtful and unhelpful. Jungian analyst Jean Shinoda Bolen writes,

> When we find that we are not loved or are loved only for what we do or what we own, power in

some form becomes a substitute, the means by which we seek the acceptance and security that love provides freely. Thus we seek to be noticed or need-ed, to be indispensable or in control.[4]

∾ *Blabbing Isn't Truth-telling!*

Blabbing is often confused with truth-telling, and it is another way that we betray the covenant between us. "In our boredom and our despair," Jean Bethke Elshtain reminds us,

> we take to the airwaves and to the streets to pro-claim the awful and ugly truth about a spouse, a friend, a lover, a parent, a child, or a despised enemy or group. And this ugly phenomenon, this eruption of publicity and substitute of publicity for that which is authentically either private or public, is now America's leading growth industry.[5]

I was recently told of a man (a disappointed lover for whom betrothal was dust and ashes) who decided that the world needed to know the truth about something he had done. In one sense, his instinct was good, but it was a pity he didn't value the old tradition of sacramental confession or even the newer one of psychotherapy. Instead he felt justified in blabbing in ways that made him feel better but hurt others. When his relationship with a married woman went sour, he took the woman's estranged husband to lunch and told him "the truth" with no thought for the woman, the children of both marriages, or the context of her life or his. The question is, was it his truth to tell in that way? He broke covenant not once but many times in unburdening himself in a self-serving way. His truth-telling was defective and damaging because it lacked the essential ingredients of contrition, compassion, and wholeness.

I have been a priest now for over thirty years and have spent many hours listening to people tell and retell the story of their lives. I, too, have told my story over and over again to confessors, spiritual directors, and psychotherapists. It is a deep human need to tell our story over and over again in various versions and editions. Perhaps the repetition is necessary because we know that we never get it quite right. Some of us put all our energy in making sure that in the version we tell we always come out on top, while others are in the wrong; others tell quite a different tale in which they are always in the wrong and others come out on top. It's hard for us to know, let alone tell, the truth about our own lives.

We naturally want to take up the bits and pieces of our lives—the hopeful and hurting jumble of events and feelings—and weave them into some kind of story that makes us feel if not good about ourselves, then at least justified. In our heads we write and revise the account of our lives all the time. The trouble is that we mistake the current rendition of our lives for objective truth that we then bring out in our encounters with others. One dangerous weapon is gossip, especially when we slant our storytelling to our advantage and tell tales about others to their detriment. It hurts us all. It breaks the covenant. It cuts us off from communion.

Donald McCullough lays down some ground-rules for truth-telling that underscore this aspect of betrothal. How does our truth-telling serve the higher truth of covenant and communion?

> Not every truth is mine to tell: a truth shared in confidence and a truth that would needlessly hurt another is not mine to tell. Not every person has the right to know the truth: some willfully distort what they hear; some use facts to bludgeon the life out of a larger, more important truth; some have blabber-

mouths with unrelenting and undiscriminating tongues. Not every time is appropriate for the truth: some seasons call for tactful silence; the day your friend's daughter dropped out of school is not the day to tell her about your daughter making the Honor Roll.[6]

Truth is a betrothing, like falling in love and keeping your word. I want to be a person of my word. And when I fail, as I do from time to time, I look for a way of beginning again, a possibility of forgiveness. To forgive is to start again. To judge is to be brought to an end. We love and learn by experiment.

Think how we have come to eat what we eat. It took generations to figure out what was good and what was bad for us. We have to do the same with ideas as we do with artichokes and avocados. We chew on, digest, and absorb ideas so that they become part of us. New knowledge has transforming power. That is why we resist it.

True wisdom—Truth with a capital T—changes us by causing an eruption inside that reconstitutes us. We don't probe truth; truth probes us and calls us into a new way of being. We fool ourselves into thinking that we can make ourselves immune from the natural and inevitable failures that are part of our living in history. We think we can get through without the stigmata of experience, the wounds of possibility and change. But passion (in both senses of the word—passion for life and passion as suffering) are the very instruments of life. This is how the lifeblood flows through us. An ancient theologian wrote, "The flesh is the hinge of salvation." Truth as covenant and communion here and now in the mess and muddle of history.

Experience of betrayal is, perhaps, the hardest of all our personal sufferings because living without the confidence of trust poisons everything. There are the little betrayals of the insecurity of our livelihood. "Nobody can feel secure in a job," writes a columnist in the London *Times*. "It is no longer a straight run to the grave."[7] And there are the deeper betrayals of friendship, sexual love, and marriage. We live with shame and blame. How much of it is our fault and how much has the mess been encoded in the situation from the beginning? What happens if you are not selected in the dance of changing partners? What if you are cast aside? What if you cannot dance anymore with this or that person? What is there left to trust? We look for healing, and if not healing, then explanations and justifications. Like those who claim to be burned-out but never caught fire, we can always find a narrative that will explain our pain and take it out on others.

∾ *The Challenge of the Neighbor*

The word to describe what we are looking for is *authenticity*. What is authentic living? For one thing, it is an intuition, a hint of meaning in our lives. But it is more than that—an openness to someone or something calling us, making a demand on us. Authentic living is not only about having purpose in our lives and living expectantly; truth-as-betrothing means that I have to be prepared to be someone of whom demands can be made. Covenants have obligations as well as privileges. No wonder we resist them. In Abraham Heschel's words, we are not only rational beings, we are *commanded* beings, too, "beings of whom demands may be made. The central problem is not: What is being? but rather: What is required of me?"[8] What is demanded of us? If you allow yourself to be fully alive, demands will be made of you. It might hurt. You will be forced to turn your drifting into pilgrimage.

Franz Rosenweig, born of non-practicing Jewish parents in the Rhineland, was a friend of the great Jewish theologian and philosopher Martin Buber. In spite of his upbringing, Rosenweig was drawn to Jewish faith yet disappointed by his experience of the practicing Jewish community. He decided to go to the synagogue for one last time at *Yom Kippur*. He was ready to throw in the towel as far as practicing Judaism was concerned. Much to his surprise, he stayed. What he discovered was the demanding truth of the *neighbor*—the immediate experience of flesh and blood. He became betrothed to each to his brothers and sisters in covenant and realized, like many before him, that we are all in the same boat on the same journey. Rosenweig came to the conclusion that reality is so constructed that we are designed for community, for communion, for betrothal. We need one another to be ourselves. He chose love over power since, if the truth be known, we are powerless to pull ourselves up by our own shoelaces. We cannot pull ourselves up out of the messes we get ourselves into.

> Each of us can only seize by the scruff whoever happens to be closest to him or her in the mire. This is the "neighbor" the Bible speaks of. And the miraculous thing is that, although each of us stands in the mire, we can each pull out our neighbor, or at least keep him or her from drowning. None of us has solid ground under our feet; each of us is held up by the neighborly hands grasping us by the scruff, with the result that we are each held up by the next person, and often, indeed most of the time, hold each other up mutually. All this mutual upholding (a physical impossibility) becomes possible only because the great hand from above supports all these holding hands by their wrists.[9]

At this point we can state three more maxims of truth:

∾ *We enter the world seeking to be loved and we settle for power when we are not loved.*

ꙮ *None of us has solid ground under our feet.*

ꙮ *There is no such thing as standing, there is only being held up.*

We need one another to be ourselves. This is Fydor Dostoyevski's point in *The Brothers Karamazov:*

> Until you have become really, in actual fact, a brother or sister to everyone, brotherhood, sisterhood, community will not come to pass. No sort of scientific teaching, no kind of common interest, will ever teach humankind to share property and privileges with equal consideration for all. Everyone will think his or her share too small and they will always be envying, complaining, and attacking one another.

The cost of breaking the covenant is living in a terrible isolation. The more we grow aware of our distinctiveness, the greater our isolation. That is why we clutch after each other with a gnawing need and imagine it is love. We are destined to disappoint one another; our loving often leads to a nightmare of anxiety. But we are not by intention creatures of surfaces. We want relationship, all of us. We want to know others. We want others to know us. A special truth comes to us when we are confronted by our own intractable mystery and the mystery of another.

Primo Levi writes of a Nazi concentration camp where a squad of guards is sorting out the tangle of corpses, washing them with hoses and transporting them to the crematorium. Amid the tangle of bodies they find a young woman who is still alive. The event is exceptional—perhaps unique. The members of the squad are perplexed. They are used to death and here is a living person. They hide her and bring her beef broth; as they question her, they learn she is sixteen years old. The trouble is that she has seen all the horror. She is a witness. She must die. In fact they all must die sooner or later. But these debased guards are transformed; they no longer have before them an anonymous flood of frightened people coming off the boxcars: instead, they have a person.

When we are confronted by a person we often do not know what to do. But many of us sense that we are in the presence of the sacred. We catch a glimpse of the holy. We become fleetingly aware of the possibility that what is really real is bound together in some kind of covenant. We realize that we are betrothed.

Aristides, a second-century philosopher and Christian apologist, described Christians this way to the Emperor Hadrian:

> They love one another. They never fail to help widows; they save orphans from those who would hurt them. If they have something they give freely to the one who has nothing; if they see a stranger, they take him home, and are happy, as though he were a real brother or sister. They don't consider themselves brothers or sisters in the usual sense, but brothers and sisters instead through the Spirit of God.

Theologian Brian K. Smith comments about this passage, "The ancient pagan world was attracted to the Christian faith not because it presented a better philosophy or offered more fascinating religious mysteries, but because it demonstrated a new kind of community."[10]

Just after World War II, a British rabbi called Lionel Blue was convener of *Beth Din,* the Reformed Jewish ecclesiastical court in England. His job was to try to apply rules, some of them archaic, to actual situations. He writes, "As we listened to our clients' stories, we realized what a gap had grown up between our pre-war religion and post-war reality." The job was somewhat restricting and claustrophobic so Rabbi Blue decided, together with a refugee friend, to found an unusual congregation that would be the mirror image of the ecclesiastical court. There were no forms to fill in and everyone was welcome regardless of their religious or marital status.

> They were all kinds, even some well-set-up Jews, pillars-of-society Jews, Jews living with Protestants, Catholics, Buddhists, and Jews who kept very non-kosher company indeed—and of course their partners came, too, and received an even bigger welcome, not to convert them but because they might feel strange. . . . To these we added a Christian evangelical choir, who were so decent that they didn't try to convert anyone there, except by being the decent Christians that they were.

This odd assortment of people included one man who said he was the Holy Spirit and locked himself in the broom closet, and some who took one look at the other members and left in disgust. "I could have cried with relief," Blue wrote. "At last I had found a temporary religious home, and Judaism was doing what it does best, turning the religious ragtag and bobtail of a big city into a family, even a sort of holy family."[11]

The truth is that we are a family, even a sort of holy family.

∾ *We enter the world seeking to be loved and we settle for power when we are not loved.*

∾ *None of us has solid ground under our feet.*

∾ *There is no such thing as standing, there is only being held up.*

∾ *We are betrothed to one another. The world is a wedding.*

~

Chapter 9

Truth as Moral Adventure

What you think of the truth depends on what you believe.

The old Shaker hymn "Simple Gifts" ends with the refrain, "To turn, turn, will be our delight till by turning, turning we come round right." What does "coming round right" involve? John Bunyan gives us a clue in *Pilgrim's Progress* when his pilgrim meets Mr. Honest on the road to the city and his new companion tells him, "Not honesty in the abstract, but Honest is my name, and I wish that my nature shall agree with what I am called." I believe there is a deep longing in all of us for that kind of integrity. The old name for it was *connatural* knowledge, which meant knowledge so much a part of a person's experience that it is a true expression of his or her nature. We want the truth to be the fire that lights up our life from within. Truth is something I want to become. I sense this longing in everyone I meet—a fleeting look in the eye telling me of the hope that, one day, who we *say* we are (and hope to become) will actually coincide with who we really are. I would, in short, like to turn out right.

Virginia Woolf wrote of the kind of "rightness" I mean when she told her fiancé of wanting a tremendous living thing that was "always alive, always hot, not dead and easy." I suspect that most of us, deep down, want just that: to have a nature that is always in harmony with whatever is calling us to be in relationship with life. Always alive, always hot, not dead and easy. We want to be committed, betrothed, and bound in freedom to each other.

The poet Anne Sexton wrote about her longing to be truly alive and about failed efforts to be her own rescuer.

> Oh, Mary,
> Gentle Mother,
> Open the door and let me in.
> A bee has stung your belly with faith.
> Let me float in it like a fish.
> Let me in! Let me in!
> I have been born many times, a false Messiah,
> but let me be born again
> into something true.[1]

Her poem speaks to our deep longing to be reborn, which echoes through the centuries. St. Simeon, a Byzantine mystic who lived in the early eleventh century, wrote of a double birth: our birth from our mother's womb and our giving birth in the Spirit to our true selves. He saw the similarities and differences between Mary giving birth to Jesus, the Word of God, and our being continually renewed by giving spiritual birth to ourselves through the Holy Spirit.

We are getting close to what the mystics meant by being so grasped by the truth that we are reborn. I want to be born again and again into something true. This may sound strange, but there is something about me that is hidden from me. The mystical tradition would call it the image of God in me. It is as if I am waiting for something to manifest itself. *Thinking* my way through to a new sense of who I am won't work. I have even tried to live in the village of Morality in order "to come round right," and found it to be the ghetto of Mortality. I am waiting for a revelation.

The Greek word for truth *(aletheia)* suggests just such a revelation or uncovering. In Greek mythology *Lethe* was the river of forgetfulness. To forget was lethal! To remember accurately was life-bearing. Truth-telling, therefore, in the sense of longing for personal integrity, has something to do with remembering, with waking up, with being fully aware. The truth becomes something we live *into* as we grow increasingly aware and become more and more awake. As integrity bringing to birth identity, the truth has moral bite. It prods me in the direction of loving and just actions while making certain types of behavior unacceptable because they lead me away from what I long to be. In short, truth calls me into a moral adventure. And morality, as we have seen, is dangerous territory. Morality is close to moralism and moralism has a deceptive ally in pietism. We are called to holiness; we are not called to think of ourselves as "holier than thou."

At the end of Umberto Eco's *The Name of the Rose,* his detective William of Baskerville confides to his student Adso that he always knew that there were certain kinds of truths. He called them "signs." We would call them scientific facts that are important in helping us live in the world with some confidence. William confesses that while he appreciated the facts of the case he was investigating, he failed to see the relation between them.

> The order that our minds imagine is like a net, or like a ladder, built to attain something. But afterward you must throw the ladder away, because you

> discover that, even if it was useful, it was meaning-
> less.... The only truths that are useful are instru-
> ments to be thrown away.[2]

The implication is that a higher truth exists, but it must be approached with reverence, love, respect, silence.

We want to live a life in which all the bits and pieces are in touch with one another, to understand the relation among the signs. For many people the world is full of signs, but they have no clue (no narrative) to show them how the signs are related to each other. Relationship and connection is the key. The "good," suggests Iris Murdoch, see life as a dense mesh of interconnections, while the "bad" see life in separate little lumps.[3] St. Augustine wrote of the "collected man," the one who is so centered that he is able to bring together the scattered self that has been fragmented by distractions, anxieties, and decep-tions. Each of us feels disconnected or "uncollected" at one time or another. Anyone who has faced the conse-quences of their loss of innocence knows the need for mercy and forgiveness. To some extent we all live at someone else's expense: somewhere in the world others' lives are diminished because of us. Our unexamined sense of entitlement means that others have less than they need to live a decent life. Pointing out this state of affairs is not to beat up on ourselves, but to do what we can to redress the balance and, where necessary, accept that life has an intractable tragic element.

To be true is to grow up and grow out in virtue, to become people who are pregnant with such qualities as honesty, courage, patience, kindness, and generosity. What an adventure! We do not always do it very well and there is *no* compromise as to the moral demand. Forgiveness makes such a life possible and bearable. The gospel truth is that we are held responsible *and* we are for-given. The two go together. Think of what life is like if we embrace the opposite, which is a life with no responsibility and no forgiveness. It would be hell, the loss of the truly human. Eventually we would compromise ourselves so much that there would be no one at home. We would become the kind of people for whom there is nothing behind the eyes.

∾ *What Are We Becoming?*

The moral life asks us what kind of people we are becoming. Every choice we make moves us towards or away from integrity. In Woody Allen's movie *Crimes and Misdemeanors,* for example, Judah is a wealthy Jewish entrepreneur, adored by his family. He takes out a contract on his mistress and has her murdered. At first he is wracked by guilt, but as time passes his conscience becomes dull and Judah begins to "forget." The question is, did he get away with it? Appearances are deceptive. No matter how dulled his conscience, Judah is still a murderer. That's the truth. Even worse, he is a murderer who has learned to live with what he has done. How? By pretending he never did it. Judah has become the kind of person who is capable of doing anything. He has no moral compass.

A friend of mine asks his students what truth they want to become by the end of their lives. He points out that they are making something of themselves everyday. Truth has something to do with all the bits and pieces of their lives in touch with each other—sometimes in harmony, sometimes in counterpoint, but always in touch. Truth, he tells them, comes to them in the form of a story and brings them to judgment and hope, crisis and possibility.

Many people fail to realize that truth-telling is full of risk. Many of us have been telling a story to ourselves and to the world about what we think is true and real for so long that we have come to believe it absolutely. Rush Limbaugh, the radio talk-show host, and many like him espouse a view of reality that seemingly allows them to know the truth. They appear to have no struggle with self-doubt. Their version of the truth—surprise! surprise!—always puts them in the right. As we have seen, it is easy to summon several little truths in the service of a great Lie even when we are unaware of it.

I want you to tell me the truth. How can I expect you to do that if I lie to myself? How can I give you my word unless I know how to keep it? My insincerities, distortions, and misinterpretations are often hidden from me. This is what I mean when I tell you that truth is something I want to become. I want to be free of the hidden impulses that undermine my pilgrimage to integrity.

It is not surprising that many seekers end up in some form of psychotherapy. At its best, psychotherapy helps us interpret ourselves more truthfully. Spiritual direction has as one of its goals the task of clarification so that the spirit can be truly radiant. I need help—the help of the wise, the help of friends—because I am in danger of misinterpreting the mystery of who I am.

T. S. Eliot wrote in his poem *The Rock,* "O my soul, be prepared for the coming of the Stranger. Be prepared for him who knows how to ask questions." The truth that really matters comes to us as a stranger who asks hard questions. Be prepared to be probed. About what? About yourself and the story you've been telling yourself about yourself. How far is it a lie? How does it enslave and imprison you? Truth-telling is supposed to set us free, but what do we know of freedom? The story we tell about it will determine our view of what is real. As we have seen, those of us who follow Jesus as the truth believe that true liberty is revealed in the arresting images of a mother with a baby and a ruined man on the gallows. How you respond to these images will tell you something about yourself and the story you believe to be true about the world and your place in it.

In David Edgar's play *Pentecost,* refugees and hostages tell each other stories in the depth of the night. Then one of the refugees protests that it will be much harder to kill the hostages, if it becomes necessary, because they have shared stories with each other. *Storytelling binds people together.* This is its magic: not only does it cross barriers, it also breaks them down. With their fund of stories and myths, these refugees and hostages discover that they have more in common than they thought, in spite of the fact that they all speak different languages, in spite of the fact that they live in a world riven by war and divided by fiercely guarded borders. The lesser truths of ethnic identity gave way to the greater truth that there is but one human heart. To know that in Africa, in Ireland, in Serbia, is to begin to bind up the wounds of the human family. Truth-telling is a compelling and difficult spiritual task. By finding a story that is faithful to the facts we are liberated to be who we truly are: children of God and brothers and sisters to everyone.

All of us live in stories that tell us who we are. Choosing a story in which to live is, therefore, serious business. Knowing which one bears the truth is a matter of faith. Many people are unaware that they are already living in a story, often a story concocted years ago—even centuries ago—by the bits and pieces of other people's experience. From these stories, some of them deeply destructive, we learn whom to trust and whom to reject, whom to love and whom to hate, whom to kill and whom to defend.

From time to time something happens to wake us up: a tragedy, a shock, a moment of joy (a new baby, a new relationship)—something to make us aware of the fragility of things and remind us we are stewards and not owners. We are guests and hosts on the planet, not Masters of the Universe. Lee Atwater was a ruthless political activist who died at the age of forty from cancer. His illness changed him and made him look with new eyes not only at his own condition, but at the society in which he lived and the circles in which he moved. Before he became sick, Atwater sensed that something was wrong with the culture and he hoped to help the Republican Party take advantage of the malaise. But his cancer helped him see that what was missing from society was missing in him— "a little heart!" "What power wouldn't I trade," he wrote, "for a little more time with my family? What price wouldn't I pay for an evening with friends? It took a deadly illness to put me eye-to-eye with that truth." In the same way, he continued, this country suffers from a "spiritual vacuum," a "tumor of the soul."

Dennis Potter, an English playwright, when he was dying very painfully, gave a final interview on British television. He had to stop every so often to take something to kill the pain. In this interview he said,

> I'm almost serene. I can celebrate life. Below my window, there's an apple tree in blossom. It's white. In looking at it, instead of saying, "Oh, that's a nice blossom," now looking at it through the window, I see the whitest, frothiest blossom that ever there could be. The now-ness, the now-ness of everything is absolutely wondrous. If you see the present tense, boy, do you see it. And boy, do you celebrate it.

I think this is what the animals give us: they glorify God simply by being. They show us that the now-ness of everything is absolutely wondrous and cannot be bought. This is the rebellion of the romantic vision: the strange act of faith setting the death of the world, and our own perhaps imminent departure, in a context of the wonder of being and the tender glory of human relationships.

What would be one of the truest things I could do? What would be an expression of my true self? I would like to be able to give the gift of my unguarded self. When I live from fear and self-preservation or greed, I render myself unavailable to levels and qualities of being human and fully alive. This is why justice is important. It is a matter of the depth of the levels of experience available to us. Fear and selfishness, injustice and cruelty, make us unavailable to the wonder and fullness of life.

In the end justice is a matter of love. Which brings us back to the issue of morality and to the mystery of how we are made righteous without being self-righteous. One of the key words of the Bible connected with covenant is *righteousness,* a word that sounds very uninviting to our ears. It is worth taking another look at this contentious word, however, because hidden within it is the conviction not so much that we are in the right but that in God things turn out right.

    ∾ *Being righteous means being who you were meant to be—your birthright as a human being and as a child of God.*

Righteousness is a gift. That is why forgiveness is part of God's plan, because when it comes to loving fully we all fail. We all break down. When it comes to the gift of the unguarded self, some of us get terribly battered by life, by others, by demons inside us. People of faith are able to accept and bear life as a moral adventure because they have an inkling that they are deeper and lovelier than they know. Moralism is to be rejected because it tends to be cruel and, worse, it leads to despair. When our attempt to be righteous on our own fails, we become pregnant either with self-hate or with a rage against the world. In our pain or arrogance lurks the need to be in the right.

Many years ago, when our children were very little, one of the girls turned to me and asked, "Will it be all right?" I wasn't sure what the "it" referred to, but her question held a kind of cosmic significance. "Will *it* be all right?" I said yes, with my fingers crossed behind my back. That desire and wonder—will everything be all right? Are you all right? Will it be all right? Truth has something to do with our wanting things to turn out *right*. One word for this "rightness" is God's *glory*. The place of glory is where everything turns out right.

To come round where we ought to be is to be in a place just right: this is what it is to be righteous. Things will come out right when we discern that life is a gift from God. It is all gift. The truly moral life begins on the other side of our accepting God's first gift to us of our own fragile selves. Life as a moral adventure begins on the *other* side of forgiveness. Only then does truth-telling become an adventure. We begin to see ourselves as actors in a love story. "Every single one of us has a good work to do in life," writes Elizabeth O'Connor. "This good work not only accomplishes something needed in the world, but completes something in us. When it is finished, a new work emerges that will help make green a desert place as well as scale another mountain inside ourselves."

O'Connor is telling us what it means to be righteous. No wonder that the Bible tells us that we have no righteousness of our own. We are in enough trouble as it is without adding inflammatory self-righteousness to the fires of human suffering. In one of his letters St. Paul reminds us that our righteousness is "as filthy rags," the apostle's way of reminding us that it is all gift.

What a joy to come down in a place just right, in the valley of love and delight. There is a "rightness" to things and it is hard won. After much pain and a deep vision of the Crucified Christ, the medieval mystic Julian of Norwich could say, "And all shall be well, and all shall be well, and all manner of thing shall be well." Things do come round right.

∾

part four

Truth as Mystery

~

Chapter 10

Wonder and Gratitude

Truth is not truth unless there go with it kindness.

There is a kind of righteousness that freezes the heart.
In E. M. Forster's novel *A Passage to India,* an Indian
doctor, Aziz, is charged with rape. He is eventually acquit-
ted because his accuser withdraws her charge, but Doctor
Aziz is not satisfied because "while relieving the Oriental
mind," writes Forster, "she had chilled it, with the result
that he could scarcely believe that she was sincere. And
indeed from his standpoint she was not. For her behavior
rested on cold justice and honesty. She had felt, while she
recanted, no passion or love for those she had wronged.
Truth is not truth in that exacting land unless there go
with it kindness." And I'd say, not in India or anywhere
else.

"Coming round right" is to see the world through the
eyes of gratitude, and gratitude is the antidote to the
"righteousness" that freezes the heart. When we think of
righteousness as a gift, we are able to look with compassion on all the "unrighteous": those for whom there seems
to be little chance of living a life of delight and joy. Think
of the millions who have very little chance of becoming

the people they are meant to be. It isn't easy for them to be grateful. The gratitude that is the primary response to the gift of life is sometimes hard won. Think of the human cost of globalization, the widening gap between those who are mobile and those who are stuck. The human community is divided between those who are travelers and welcome everywhere—think of the Microsoft motto, "Where do you want to go today?"—and the vagabonds and wanderers who are welcome nowhere.[1]

Think of the escalating incarceration of people around the world: the criminalization of poverty globally, with new forms of social control over increasingly large segments of the population for which there is no longer work, meaning, or opportunity to love in a humane manner. In many parts of the world, there is not much chance of being righteous or of becoming what you are meant to be. Moreover, to tell people that they *should* be grateful is, in many cases, a cruel and useless exercise. This dilemma adds urgency to our seeing life as a moral adventure in which our commitment to truth becomes a commitment to action, to responsibility. It is only when we see the whole world as the place of God's gift that will we work for the "righteousness" of all of God's family. There is no "private" righteousness; we're all in this together.

What are the ingredients of the righteousness that leads to gratitude? One is the need to be needed, while another is the need to be connected to the life of passion. A third, deceptively simple, is kindness, a generous receptivity toward others.

There were reports during the Second World War of the siege of Leningrad. "Living in the cold, hungry, dark city, people held themselves together by the consciousness of being needed," says one commentator. "They began to die when they had nothing to do." Having nothing to do was more terrible than a bombing raid. The human need to be needed is more powerful, we are told, than the need to survive. I am not sure that is true, but it makes me think. It convinces me that the second ingredient of "righteousness" is indeed passion, an allegiance to someone or something larger than oneself. Passion is an essential ingredient to the fully human and, therefore, "righteous" life. Without a generous outlet, our passion goes rancid.

I have been fortunate to know the author Sam Keen, who has a fully-rigged trapeze in his garden in Sonoma, California, and sponsors a trapeze school. Recently, I watched a group of adults and children practice together the art of flying. Trapeze requires trust, teamwork ("Never fly alone"), and the ability to fall skillfully. Trapeze artists have a great deal to teach about the life of passionate faith, and I wrote the following poem after watching Sam do his workout high above the safety net. To my amazement and gratitude, new truths about myself and this marvelous world began to reveal themselves. I realized afresh that trust and truth go together and that risk has more to do with "righteousness" than with following rules. In fact, there is nothing more tragic than the walled-up heart playing only for safety.

Trapeze

Sam, his callused hands
Protected by gauze and thongs
Flies and tumbles into the net
Teaching himself to fall.
Without something like this, he said,
Passion turns rancid.

I wonder what trapeze
Is waiting to keep my passion fresh?
What safety net will break my fall?
What grace can stand the stench of

Passion long deferred?

In one scenario I know
The broken bones rejoice.
The victim reigns
Stretched out for all to see
On Adam's tree.

When I swung on the rope this morning
My arms were weak.
The mind hoped for something easy—
A little yoga
To see if the spirit still bubbles
In the ruins
Where we once lived?

Fresh bread and wine—
Signs, after all, of passion—
Purify the air and feed me
As I am turned into the breathing image
Under my own big top.
Stretched high,
I am caught—mid-air—
By the catcher's strong arms.

Watching people practice on Sam's trapeze, including a six-year-old girl full of trust and confidence, I recovered my own longing to give myself away. We long to let go. That's what it is to be human. We long to come down where we ought to be. And where ought we to be? In a place just right in the valley of love and delight where the heart sings. Righteousness and gratitude begin to emerge when we care for truth in such a way that patience, self-restraint, generosity, candor, and a willingness to be taught courage come to the fore.

∾ *The Sky is Falling! The Sky is Falling!*

Is everything coming to an end? There are many telling us that the end is near, which is why I am comforted by the cartoon of a bearded prophetic figure carrying a placard that reads: "The world is *not* coming to an end and we're going to have to cope!" But how are we going to cope? The world is full of horror and wonder and it doesn't take much to tip the scales one way or the other with regard to the way we see the world. Sometimes I am filled with wonder, sometimes I am filled with dread. I am trying to cope. On the one hand, there is a feeling of disintegration and fragmentation and on the other a promise of new wholeness.

One Thanksgiving we bought a new VCR and on the unit was a sticker that read, "Be smart. Read your manual first. Save trouble later." I have tended to live my life on the principle of "When all else fails, read the instructions." This warning made me think of the challenge of being human. None of us comes into this world with an instruction manual, although once we see the light of day there are numerous "instructions" or texts that are ready to tell us how to live our lives, from do-it-yourself books to sacred stories claiming divine inspiration. Being without a manual is all right when times are more or less stable and we can simply conform, go with the flow. Truth is not an issue. But when things are up for grabs we tend to hang on to anything that might give us a clue to what's going on.

Apocalypse is in the air and its effect on us is often toxic, with its destabilizing reminders of our vulnerability and mortality. The world is remarkably shaky and we feel it personally. When I fly to New York next week, will a maniac have planted a bomb on the plane? When I go to that concert on Tuesday, will I be killed or maimed? When my son travels on the subway, will he come up to street-level alive? These are no longer fanciful questions, even if most of us go on with our lives and rightly refuse to be ruled by fear. But it is no use pretending that somewhere deep inside us we remain untouched by instability. There is danger of spiritual and moral paralysis in the expectation of apocalypse—especially of our personal apocalypse. How much of this is in our heads? How much say do we have in our destiny? How do we cope without a manual, without a moral and spiritual compass? The guiding star is wonder, amazement, and gratitude.

I am struck by the simple fact that my day goes better when I begin it with a pause for a moment of astonishment. If I am lucky, this sense of amazement is sustained by gratitude. I am amazed that there is a day at all, that there is a "me" to live it. I am full of wonder that there is *anything,* even a depressed and faithless me. A sense of wonder is the beginning of prayer. Wonder is the bedrock of mature belief as well as the soil out of which trust grows.

∾ *Secrets of the Heart*

Recently I met a woman who had led a full life and enjoyed several successful careers in the arts. Famous literary figures had passed through her house during her childhood and Ernest Hemingway had taken her to her first bull fight. Affluent, successful, and cultivated, she said to me, "I wake up early in the morning and hear the voice of my dead mother saying to me, 'Get out of my sight! You make me sick!'" Across seventy years of memory the cruel voice insists on telling and retelling its terrible lie. At eighty my new friend wanted to change her life and rewrite her life story so that she could, at last, find herself. Until now she had seen the world through the prism of her tears, dictated by a cruel remark made decades earlier by her mother. As a child she had been lied to about who she really was, but now the truth about her was beginning to emerge. She was finally accepting the fact that she was deeper and lovelier than she had ever known.

Many things have an impact on our hearts: an unkind word said decades ago, the death of a child, the news of cancer, the break-up of a long relationship. It is easy to believe that our own experiences are *literal* representations of the truth. It is a terrible thing to be the victim of someone else's interpretation of our own experience and to find ourselves a character in someone else's drama. Over the years, I have received hundreds of letters from people telling me of their experiences (including those of me) as if these experiences were objectively true, yet these accounts usually tell me more about my correspondents' own interpretations than about the experiences themselves. If you were to read my journal, for example, you would get a very distorted picture of my life because I only write in it when I am feeling low. It is hard for us to understand that experiences are not "facts," but a mixture of events and interpretation. That is why autobiography is so difficult to write: we have to honor our experiences but at the same time be aware of the fact that the *way* we interpret them is a construct, an invention. Is there a way out of this dilemma? Wonder and gratitude can lead us through the muddle and mess of conflicting interpretations and into a more generous way of looking at the world.

Why not have a benign view of the world? For example, what comes to mind when you hear, "Twinkle, twinkle little star"? Do you remember how it made you feel? Philosopher Martha Nussbaum tells the story of one of her students who was asked this question. He saw a sky beautifully blazing with stars and bands of bright color, and the sight made him look in a new way at his dog, a cocker spaniel.

I used to look into the dog's eyes and wonder what the dog was really thinking and feeling. Was my dog ever sad? It pleased me to think about my dog and the way he experienced the world. I looked him in the eyes and knew that he loved me and was capable of feeling pleasure and pain. It then made me think tenderly about my mom and dad and other children I knew.

Why would "Twinkle, twinkle little star" make someone think that the starry sky was benevolent and not malevolent? Why think of your dog as loving and good rather than devilish and cruel? Who cares whether a dog is happy or sad? But Martha Nussbaum assures us that something important is going on. "The strange fact is," she writes,

> that the nursery rhyme itself, like other rhymes, nourishes a tender humanity within us and stirs up in us the prospect of friendship. It doesn't make us think paranoid thoughts of a hateful being in the sky who's out to get us. It tells the child to think of a star as a diamond rather than as a missile of destruction. . . . The nursery rhyme nourishes a generous construction of the seen.[2]

In times of upheaval, how we choose to interpret experience becomes especially crucial because to choose "doom and gloom" as a way of seeing the world becomes a self-fulfilling prophecy. If I see the world as a hopeful place, I will behave accordingly. As we have seen, what we believe is true and whether we view the world with cynicism or hope depends not only on our experience, but on the stories we choose to tell in interpreting it.

For example, two men can have what appear to be an identical experience of grinding childhood poverty with a brutal father and a long-suffering mother. One man sinks into the experience and the other rises above it. Why?

There are many factors that contribute to the different ways we choose to interpret experience: one of them is that elusive thing called character; others are timing and chance. But one vital factor is the *story* we choose to tell ourselves about the meaning of our experiences. It makes all the difference if we choose a generous construction of what we see. If astonishment is the beginning of prayer, choosing a generous view of the world and living gratefully are the seeds of faith, hope, and love—the bedrock of what is true.

When we wake up in the morning, we can see the world through a variety of prisms. If we are truly aware, we will have glimpsed some terrible truths: that life is often hard, that we are going to die, that we are not in control. It is at that point of recognition that we have a choice. Far from being depressing, such knowledge of our frailty can be the occasion of liberation, even hilarity. Amazement and gratitude can put us in touch with purposes and possibilities larger than ourselves. It comes as a relief not to find ourselves at the center of the universe.

Believing in destiny rather than fate is a gamble of faith worth taking. Human beings are choosing animals. So why not choose to do good rather than evil, to choose a generous view of the world rather than a crabbed one? I value Martin Luther's attitude, who was supposed to have said, "If I knew the world was going to end tomorrow, I'd plant an apple tree today."

Where does the trouble lie? We lose touch with our own mystery and try to live in a smaller, more manageable world than the real one. St. Augustine's "unstable heart" *(cor inquietum)* throws us off balance and pushes us toward a truth for which we long without knowing what it is. We are drawn to and baffled by mystery. Karl Jaspers once wrote that Augustine thought in questions. Augustine was a tireless seeker, sailing, like his hero Aeneas, toward ever-receding shores. Augustine said,

"Since it is God we are speaking of, you do not understand it. If you could understand it, it would not be God."
Gary Wills comments, "We seek one mystery, God, with
another mystery, ourselves. We are mysterious to ourselves
because God's mystery is in us." As Augustine put it, "Our
mind cannot be understood, even by itself, because it is
made in God's image."[3]

In *Love is Stronger than Death*, Cynthia Bourgeault
speaks to those moments in personal relationships when
no matter what one does, hurt and pain are the result. It
helped me make sense of my own journey, which so often
seemed full of failure.

> The deepest side of intimacy is that we *are* invited
> inside the other; as love follows its natural
> path.... We stand in the midst of one another's
> dragons, which must be regarded with infinite ten-
> derness and compassion. To look upon them with
> loathing is a kind of inner murder, like the fox
> minding the henhouse. Where such murder is quiet-
> ly taking place under the guise of relationship, the
> partners gradually become outer shells, trapped
> more and more in their personalities and increas-
> ingly numb on the inside. The dragons recede deep-
> er and deeper into the unconscious.[4]

When I feel in the grip of failure in my relationships, I
ask myself, "Who are you on your way to becoming? Do
you seek one mystery, God, with another mystery, yourself?" I am convinced that we are in a time when basic definitions of what it means to be human are being
renegotiated, including definitions of our faith-journey.
Human history can be interpreted as one story of exclusion after another as people try to get into the human conversation. Some do it angrily and noisily; others take over
the conversation and make sure those who formerly dominated it are pushed to the edges. Youth is silenced by age

and then youth takes its revenge. One race or tribe domi-
nates another and then the roles are reversed. Men lord it
over women and women seek to turn the tables. The married look upon the unmarried as second-class, wounded,
and incomplete. "Why can't you be like us? Why can't you
be 'normal'?" Or the religious community, by invoking in
a twisted way the biblical witness, make the single state
into a curse or misinterpret it as a "higher" calling.

The trick is to learn to make judgments without
becoming judgmental. That is quite an art. It does not
mean that we are never to be critical and confrontational,
but let's be critical with some self-knowledge and compassion. A great medieval Muslim poet wrote, "If we looked
for God instead of gold, you wouldn't see a single blind
man beside the ditch." Which holds the greater truth?
God or gold? God calls us into covenant, not with death,
but with each other, in humility and love.

Perhaps we should end by coming back to wonder and
gratitude for our own fragile selves. In *Grace Abounding*
John Bunyan wrote: "I was more loathsome in mine own
eyes than was a toad, and I thought I was so in God's eyes,
too: sin and corruption would as naturally bubble out of
my heart as water would bubble out of a fountain." He
lived in this torment and self-hatred until he heard a sermon on the text: "Behold thou art fair, my love, thou are
fair." The words "my love" stuck in his mind, and Bunyan
went home repeating, "Thou art my love, thou art my
love, thou art my love," believing that God meant these
words for him. He had, at last, heard the truth about himself and it was wonderful.

∾

Chapter 11

The Music of Trust

*The poverty or richness of our loving determines
what is real.*

I remember with gratitude and affection my training as a
choir boy in the great English tradition of choral music.
It changed and shaped my life. Years later, I am convinced
that the music has influenced the way I approach and
think about the truth as a way of trusting life as a gift.
Music has the capacity for a multiplicity of moods and
meanings, undermining our narrow certainties even as it
sustains and nourishes us. For me, music, more than any
other art form, bears the truth in all its disturbing and sustaining openness and pushes me toward a spontaneous
"Thank you!" for life. Each of us has, perhaps, a piece of
music that speaks to us more deeply than any words. I
think of the *Incarnatus* from one of Palestrina's masses,
which contains fifty seconds of music that deepens and
strengthens my "yes" to life in a way that I cannot
explain. Music speaks to me of three basic human issues
having to do with trust: thoughts of death, the desire for
happiness, and the reality of love. When I hear a great
piece of music, I appreciate once more my own instability

136

in a changing world and am challenged to reevaluate what really matters.

Music may seem a strange way to introduce our need for developing a community of trust. I like the music metaphor because being a musician means learning a craft, one that requires the skill of paying attention to others in such a way that a group (an orchestra or a quartet) can truly play *in concert*. When I watch others make music it is like overhearing a great conversation. The musicians pay attention to each other in a reverential pattern of harmony and counterpoint. Above all they complete a circle of delight—delighting in the music, delighting in each other, delighting in delighting. In short, they enjoy each other.

Stephen Carter, the cultural critic and law professor, laments:

> We have lost our talent for conversation. What argument is about today is waiting for your chance to show the other fellow that he is an idiot. Nobody says anymore what is for me a vital part of my creed: "I may disagree with what you say but I'll fight to the death for your right to say it." Instead, people say, "I disagree with what you say, and you're a monster for having said it," or "It should be against the law to say it." This is a horrible thing.[1]

Carter was clerk to Thurgood Marshall in 1980 and claims that he learned three lessons from the Supreme Court justice. First, never lose sight of the fact that what we call the law affects real people. It is never an abstraction. Second, be true to your convictions and say what you believe no matter what others may think. Third and most important of all, the fact that someone disagrees with you doesn't make him or her an enemy.

All three lessons require a community of trust. Think for a moment about the law and its application. Without the mediating influence of a community of trust, the law is a cruel and blunt instrument. Applying the law "equally," without reference to responsibility and circumstances, is unjust. Think what happens to trust when we are not true to our convictions, when we do not mean what we say and say what we mean. Think how impossible life becomes when we use excommunicating rhetoric against those with whom we disagree. There is no way we can make music together.

∾ *Barriers to Trust*

What are the barriers to developing an ever-widening radius of trust? First of all is the barrier of an impoverished imagination that can neither be taken by surprise nor say "Thank you!" One form of this impoverishment is the madness of the view that we have absolutely *nothing* in common. The name for this is *incommensurability* and it says that the differences between us are so great that they cannot be measured. "There is no point in our talking with each other. My view of the world has no room for the likes of you and your view of the world could not possibly make room for me." Such an attitude makes true conversation impossible. There is no way we can play "in concert."

There is little we can do, furthermore, when we are faced with a conversation stopper, such as the bumper sticker that reads, "The Bible says it. I believe it. That settles it!" The Bible settles nothing. Rather, it unsettles. There are other conversation stoppers, too, like "I'm white. You're black. I'm straight and you're gay. I'm male. You're female. We have nothing to say to each other. Besides, you just don't *get* it, you *can't* get it, and you never will!" Are we all irrevocably stuck inside our own skins? Can I be reduced to my membership of a race, an ethnic group, or sex? Does this do me justice? Is this who I am? This endless pursuit of identity kills any possibility that you and I might be *more* than we know. If instead we were to pursue integrity more vigorously, then identity would follow.

Truth-telling requires the ability to argue, to disagree without being disagreeable, to be skilled at counterpoint as well as harmony. Argument is good, but in our culture it is very hard simply to have a good fight. We commit the sin of "totalism" (admitting nothing outside our little world—our truth) and construct a cosmos of no compromise. Truth itself, as well as community, becomes "balkanized" into competing claims made by special interest groups. We cannot imagine a commonwealth in which *all* have an interest.

As pilgrims we are called to reimagine the world as hospitable to life, to recover its sacred identity. Every metaphor, of course, has its weaknesses. How can we be many and yet one? The image of the human race as a great quilt might serve as we move through the painful process of acknowledging the sometimes terrible differences occasioned by race, gender, and class into the kind of world where we are judged by the content of our character rather than the color of our skin. Can we imagine a world in which there is enough *trust* to allow someone quite different from us to watch out for our interests? Must my representative at the public table be white and male? Must yours be black and lesbian? Must hers be Latino and his Asian? And what about all the people who are left out of these categories?

Can we trust the fact that a culture is made up of many voices, all which are called to join in a conversation, an endless unrehearsed symphony in which we play with such confidence and trust that the dissonances do not frighten us and the fact that the symphony is never finished delights rather than dismays us? Is this asking too much of people? Are we up to such a work of the mind and heart that we can imagine new possibilities for the human race? Can we live in a world subject to constant disruption, even if it happens to be the real world? No wonder we are always trying to invent a more stable one. But "reality" itself is unstable and subject to the penetration of the imagination. Some of us ask, "Why not manufacture a manageable world devoid of ambiguity?" Why risk the uncertainties of the real world when we have the power and know-how to *invent* one?

Politicians with an ideological bent would like to legislate programs of social engineering that bring into being a more perfect world. The wealthy often use their money to invent the world they want to live in. Money cannot keep the real world at bay (the plane may blow up, the bomb may go off in the restaurant) but it can do a great deal to create a world that can stay stable just long enough for me to live safely until I die.

The worlds of the rich and poor collide in death. Sometimes they meet in other ways. Many of the wealthy understand that they are stewards, not owners, and use their money for the common good. The world becomes more "true" as the gap between the rich and poor narrows. It becomes less and less stable as the gap widens.

There are, however, means other than wealth to construct a virtual world of stability and certainty. Religion is also used to build fortresses. For many of us, the promise that there is no ambiguity, that there are final solutions and right answers, comes as a breath of fresh air. That may be true, but this "breath of fresh air" comes at a price: the lowering of consciousness that is itself a kind of servitude. Our freedom is diminished when we harness ourselves to a lie. We all, then, are reduced to playing in an orchestra with a limited repertoire and only one kind of instrument.

A world in which there is no ambiguity is untrustworthy because it has no need of the life of the imagination. In such a world, in fact, imagination is the enemy. If everything is settled, new vision comes as a threat. In the name of liberty we embrace a tight, manageable world in which our social contexts get smaller and human possibilities are put on hold. We do need limits and boundaries, but too easily they become prisons and barricades. It takes more maturity than most of us can muster to be able to take differences in our stride and not be driven crazy by lack of closure on crucial issues. We live by custom and habit, and often these quietly and effectively kill trust by dampening the fires of the imagination.

Another barrier to trust is our confusion about how we are to treat one another. When does helping someone amount to interfering with them? When is intervention on behalf of another called for, and when is "doing good" no more than harmful patronizing? Acts of subtle but real violence are perpetrated in the name of knowing what is best for someone else. On a community level, we do harm for the best of motives, or we go to the opposite extreme and justify callous indifference in the name of leaving people alone. We even find moral argument in limiting acts of kindness: "I'd like to help you but it would be bad for your character!" Working through such issues takes time and imagination and, as we have seen, these are in short supply. The weakness of democracy is that nothing is finally settled. Issues are always having to be revisited and renegotiated. The music is capable of endless variation.

At the same time we are experiencing instability and disintegration, a new set of allegiances is emerging that transcend national boundaries. For example, on a flight from Dallas to New York I sat next to a Frenchwoman who lived in New York and represented a French company owned by Americans. She was definitely French but she was more than that—a member of a new breed for whom national boundaries were becoming meaningless. I felt a great affinity with her world without boundaries, but I wondered how she managed and ordered her allegiances. What sort of people do we need to become in order to survive and flourish in this new millennium? Have we the will to *imagine* a world that can construct boundaries and yet have the wisdom to transcend them, when necessary, in the service of a widening vision of community?

Let's look at some of the ways we inhibit the building of trust based on our perceptions of geography. What does the United States look like from the west coast? What does California look like from the midwest? For much of the rest of the country, San Francisco is a hotbed of raving and irresponsible liberalism; for others, the state of Texas is a hotbed of intolerant fundamentalists. The media enlarges, exaggerates, and distorts our differences. Television images of the excesses of the Gay Freedom Day Parade in San Francisco are beamed into the homes of middle America and help reinforce the extravagant stereotypes. The bombing in Oklahoma City, the shootings in Littleton and Atlanta, saddened but did not surprise anyone in the liberal enclaves of the west coast. In Oklahoma, after all, they love "guns and God" so of course they are prone to violence. So runs the thinking. We exile each other with such comments as, "I don't see how any intelligent person could possibly believe *that!*" Or, "What do you expect from people like that?" How hurtful even an apparently innocent remark can be. This aggressive style of human encounter afflicts all aspects of our common life and threatens an already fragile ability to trust.

∾ *Democracy: An Exercise in Trusting Strangers*
Among other things, democracy relies on a scrupulous honesty with regard to the use of language. We need to watch the words we thoughtlessly use because they reveal deep-seated prejudices and presuppositions. Democracy is

threatened when language is abused and manipulated. The music of democracy takes practice.

What happens when we risk astonishment, gratitude, and trust? We are liberated to embrace a change of heart. The religious words for this liberating change are repentance (being capable of a change of mind) and compunction (willingness to have one's heart touched). They provide the protocols against abuse and manipulation, healing the imagination by restoring its freedom. The capacity to feel sorry for what we have done and the grace to admit it provide the public debate with the lucidity it needs to go forward. As Gil Bailie writes in *Violence Unveiled,* "Contrition is the specifically Christian form of lucidity."[2]

Democracy (which is a way of defining an open and inclusive public conversation) requires citizens who can repent and feel sorrow, who can admit their mistakes and not gloss over their shameful acts. Democracy needs citizens who are committed to telling the truth even if they seldom get it quite right. It is our seldom "getting it right" that necessitates the ongoing conversation. John Gardner writes: "The play of conflicting interests in a framework of shared purposes is the drama of a free society. It is a robust exercise and a noisy one, not for the faint-hearted or the tidy-minded."[3] Diversity, therefore, isn't merely a "good thing." Without it there is little hope of renewal and adaptation in a world that is rapidly changing. The faint-hearted and the tidy-minded are not given to astonishment and find it hard to trust.

Amazement, gratitude, and trust are religious categories. They raise the issue of faith and how we think about truth. We are at yet another watershed with regard to the very nature of the religious enterprise. Human spiritual projects are ambiguous, stirring up hatred and hope, division and inclusion. For example, there is a great divide between those who understand religion as a way of

enforcing tribal behavior and those who see it as a journey
in faith. There are also new configurations and allegiances, marked by idiosyncratic spiritualities. There are
Roman Catholics who believe in reincarnation and
Buddhists who attend mass. I met a witch for the first time
a few years ago. She came from a Jewish background,
loved the earth, and saw divinity in the local and in the
particular—in trees and streams. I liked her. More important, I trusted her and we got on well. We are all on the
move and are finding ourselves with fellow-pilgrims
unimagined a few years ago.

The fastest growing group of religious people is made
up of the unaffiliated: those who are bypassing the tradi-
tional denominations in order to lead a different kind of
spiritual life and make a different kind of music. And
given the state of much American religion, who can blame
them? In fact, many believe that the last place to find a
nurturing spirituality is in institutional religion. This is an
unfair but prevailing perception. For as I read the material on business leadership and meet various corporate lead-
ers, issues of spirituality and values are always in the
center of the conversation but it would occur to very few
of them that the religious community would be the place
to find such issues intelligently addressed. When it comes
to talking about religion, we are at cross purposes.

I meet two sets of people between whom is a great gulf.
On one side are the narrowly tribal and on the other those
who see the world (indeed, the universe) as a vast, inter-
connecting message system. The tribal people tend to find
their identity exclusively in race, gender, and class. They
cling to differences, while the other group emphasizes
what human beings have in common. Not all tribal aspi-
rations are negative, of course. To be proud of one's heritage, to enjoy ethnic foods and preserve ethnic customs,
adds color and texture to the music. It is when the tribal
becomes the only lens through which we can see the world

that we get into trouble. Conversation and music-making become difficult across this gulf. It is not simply a problem with civility and good manners, but has more to do with a lack of trust in language itself—the building blocks of imagination. Our words do not carry our meanings in the way they once did. Too many things are up for grabs. That is why we are more easily captivated by crippling fantasies than enlarged by broadening visions.

One of our problems has to do with the word "community" itself. To some it suggests a too narrowly defined group bound together by shared beliefs and heritage. "Community" tends to be defined by those who see it as repressive and redefined by those who see it as liberating. A community has to have boundaries, but these must be porous enough to allow for open and disciplined conversation. How diverse can a community be before it disintegrates into factions? Radical individualists tend to see community as repressive, but how we see ourselves and the human community is always a matter of choice. We have already asked ourselves, "What makes some people choose a generous construction of the *seen*? And why do others refuse depth, wonder, and possibility?"

Wonder, gratitude, civility, imagination—all helps us make music together. In the end, trust is a matter of seeing the unique beauty and possibility in others. It is God-given. An old name for it is the image of God. Seeing this image takes practice.

There is a story that the angels were envious when God made human beings in the divine image. So they conspired to hide the image of God where no man or woman would think to look for it. "How about in the depths of the ocean?" one suggested. "No, at the top of a high mountain would be better," said another. But the shrewdest of the angels had the best idea of all. "Let us hide the divine image in the heart of each man and woman. That is the last place they'd look for it."

The image of God is our "instrument." It is there in all of us, but we have to know where to look for it. When we find it, we find we can trust it. When we trust it, truth is revealed in all its integrity and radiance. We can make music.

∾

The Kingdom of Love and Truth

The world is a wedding and we are all invited.

We have come a long way in moving from truth as fact to truth as trust. We have had to pass through the realm of fiction because facts need stories, and we have looked for stories that are faithful to the facts. One of A. N. Wilson's characters in his novel *Daughters of Albion* puts it well: "We inhabit a world of facts, a world where things either are, or are not, the case, where events did or did not happen; but facts and events actually possess no significance *until they have been lit up by the imagination.*"[1] We end with the knowledge that the full truth cannot be understood without love, and love is not love without forgiveness. Truth. Love. Forgiveness. These three are the ingredients of the air we breathe if we are to be true to who we really are. They allow us to make music together.

◌ *A Story*

Once upon a time there was a holy rabbi who was granted a vision of the last judgment, when the human race was on trial. He found himself in a courtroom in which there was a table, and on it were the scales of justice. There were also two doors, both of them open. Through one he could see the light of Paradise, through the other the darkness of Hell. The defense counsel entered the courtroom carrying only a small bundle of good deeds under his arm—it had not been a great year for good deeds. Next, the chief prosecutor came in with two assistants, each carrying an enormous sack of sins. Dropping their sacks before the scales of justice, they took a deep breath, and went back for more. "This isn't even a tenth of it," they said, as they dragged in more sacks. The defense counsel, whose tiny bundle of good deeds looked pathetic indeed next to the great pile of sins sitting on the floor, buried his head in his hands and sighed.

Just outside the door to Paradise someone was listening. It was Levi Yitzhak of blessed memory, the rabbi of Berditshev. When he was on earth, this rabbi had sworn that not even in death would he forget the plight of struggling humanity. When he heard the sigh of the defense counsel, he decided to slip into the court room. Seeing the tiny bundle of good deeds next to the huge sacks of sins, Levi Yitzhak didn't take long to size up the situation. Waiting until there was a recess, and the courtroom was empty, he began to drag the sacks of sins one at a time to the door leading to Hell. It took all his strength and a great deal of time to throw them in one by one. He was almost finished—in fact he was holding the very last sack—when the prosecutors and the defense counsel returned. Rabbi Yitzhak was caught red-handed. He did not deny what he had done. How could he? He had thrown away the sins so that the good deeds would outweigh the bad.

Since the court was bound to uphold the law, the chief prosecutor demanded justice. "It is written that a thief shall be sold for his theft. Let Levi Yitzhak be sold at auction right now in this courtroom! Let's see if anyone will bid for him."

By now the demons from Hell and the angels from Heaven had heard all the commotion in the courtroom and they came to watch the two parties lined up beside the scales of justice. The bidding began. Abraham, Isaac, and Jacob threw their good deeds onto the scales and the matriarchs added theirs. All of the righteous contributed what they could, but the dark forces were able to gather up numberless sins stored in the deep places of the earth. The scale on their side went down and down and down. Rabbi Yitzhak was doomed. His crime had been to throw away the sins of the world so that we could be forgiven. "I buy him!" said the chief prosecutor, and dragged him to the door leading to the great darkness.

Just then, above the courtroom, from the Throne of Glory itself, came a voice. "I buy him!" There was a great silence. And God spoke, "I buy him. Heaven and Earth are mine, and I give them all for Levi Yitzhak, who would have me forgive my children."[2]

❧ The Kingdom of God

One of the most pressing issues of our time is the need for a new social and political vision that transcends the old rhetoric of left and right. The New Testament calls for a drastic reimagining of the human project in the light of the reign of God. The idea of the kingdom of God probes and undermines our concepts of power and revolutionizes our vision of what it is to be human. The truth is that we are only truly ourselves in relationship, in covenant, in communion. In a recent sermon the theologian Rebecca Parker remarked that "to have a soul is to live rooted in knowing and feeling that we are connected to one another and to the earth, that our life is held in an embrace of something larger than ourselves." But we easily become anesthetized, which brings the slow paralysis of surprise. God's "method" always takes us by surprise.

There are several surprising images of God's kingdom in the gospels. Take Matthew's parable of the mustard seed, the tiniest of all the seeds, which when it has grown is "the greatest of shrubs and becomes a tree, so that the birds of the air come and make nests in its branches" (13:32). It speaks of the leverage of smallness. The truth of the reign of God is about the true nature of power. It is found in unexpected places and resides in the humility of great-hearted human beings. At the end of *How the Irish Saved Civilization,* Tom Cahill provides us with a vision of the truth of the kingdom of God as sustained by what the world would regard as "tiny seeds." He suggests that the affluent and powerful are the Romans of the twenty-first century and compares the Roman roads to our communications system. But he warns us that

> that road system became impassable rubble, as the empire was overwhelmed by population explosions beyond its borders. So will ours. Rome's demise instructs us in what inevitably happens when impoverished and rapidly expanding populations, whose ways and values are only dimly understood, press up against a rich and ordered society.... Perhaps history is always divided into Romans and Catholics—or, better, catholics. The Romans are the rich and powerful who run things their way and must always accrue more because they instinctively believe that there will never be enough to go around; the catholics, as their name implies, are universalists who instinctively believe that all humanity makes one family, that every

human being is an equal child of God, and that God will provide.[3]

Yeast is still another image that the gospels use for the kingdom; it works in secret, like the yeast in bread-making. The kingdom is also like a *treasure* that is hidden in a field, so that we must know where our heart truly is. It challenges us to reorder our values. The kingdom is a *pearl* of great price, which implicitly asks us what is worth living and dying for. Finally, the kingdom is a *net,* which speaks to the movement of all things toward a certain end and promises a final judgment.

Final judgment? How does God's truth judge us? We will be judged in the light of how far we have lived as people betrothed to each other. We will be judged in the light of the truth that being is communion. James Baldwin speaks not only for African-Americans but for all of us when he writes of living in a country in which black people have given up "all hope of communion," a country in which black and white people do not dare even to look at each other. Without true communion we are captive to a great lie. The kingdom is about communion and about mending what has been broken.

Here is a story of how the mystery of God's reign works. A young man came home to Iowa after the Second World War. His mother and sisters waited for him—the only veteran to return alive to that town. The band played. The mayor was there. But the man who climbed off the train was not the lively, cheerful boy who had left. He was a ghost. He didn't register recognition of any one—mother, sister, or friend. His family took him to the farm and he sat in the old rocking chair in the parlor. He did not speak or move. He hardly ate. In that state for days, then weeks, and months. No one in the town had heard of traumatic shock, but they did know that his soul was lost somewhere.

His sister stayed by his side and talked. She told him about the church potluck, who was there, what they ate, and what each young woman wore. She told him the bits of news she heard in town when she went shopping and how the crops were doing. She told him how the wind had blown the clean laundry into the tomatoes. When she ran out of things to say, she'd just sit with him, snapping beans, mending socks. And he sat there, silent, like a stone.

One night, while she was sitting quietly with him, knitting, she looked over and saw that tears were falling from his eyes. She put her arm around him and then he began to let the tears flow. They came out of him like a wailing torrent, great sobs of anguish and a bellowing from deep inside him. The sister was the yeast—she saw in her ghostly brother the pearl of great price.

Then he began to talk and would not stop—of the cold, the fear, the noise, the death of his buddies, the long marches, and then the people in the camps, the mass graves, the smell. He went on all night until the story was told. His sister made him breakfast and he went out and did the morning chores. This is how the truth of the reign of God comes to us.

∾ The Cross Tests Everything

Discerning the right relationship between authority, truth, and freedom is crucial for sharing in God's reign. Whose authority should we follow and how should it be exercised? Are there absolute values? Absolute truths? And if there are, how are they to be expressed and implemented? Can we be bullied into truth, or must we discover it for ourselves through trial and error? Can truth be forced on anyone? *Crux probat omnia,* "the cross tests everything." In the light of the cross truth by its very nature is humble, strong only in terms the world can scarcely understand.

There are many political and social issues behind the question of how the truth is expressed in action. Freedom *is* a problem: how can you be free in such a way that you are truly yourself? Two slaveries torment us: slavery to the will of others and slavery to our own inner impulses. How might you be master or mistress over yourself? That's the trick. I say to myself, "I don't know what I want, but I want it *now.*" The nagging and maddening voice in a consumer society: *I want! I want! I want!* We hope that something or someone will tell us who we are and where we are going.

At the beginning of our exploration into the mystery of truth we met John, lost in his drinking. John had to make the most important journey of all—the long journey inward. John saw that he could not live out the truth of who he was without entering the citadel of himself to discover what was inside. To his surprise, John found the image of God withing himself, which freed him to face without despair the mess he had made of things.

Centuries of human cruelty and folly teach us that you cannot have true freedom without regard for the *authority* of truth. The odd thing is that you cannot be truly free until you have surrendered to some kind of authority. The great spiritual task is to find the authority that truly liberates. Is there an allegiance that can liberate? Is there one whose service is perfect freedom?

The Christian religion claims that Jesus Christ is the final authority concerning what is real. We claim that Jesus Christ has *universal* significance, which, of course, makes him a stumbling block, a scandal, a joke to many. Being willing to go on a spiritual adventure for the sake of truth helps us sort out our desires, our addictions, and our commitments. We uncover, sometimes to our shame, where our attention truly lies—in fear and in self-preservation. What we attend to most shapes our souls. It is then that we learn that truth and freedom go together; you cannot have one without the other. Our truth is Christ. We go further: we claim that Christ is *the* Truth "whose service is perfect freedom." What are we saying? What about other religious traditions? What about those people who are not remotely Christian? If Christ has a claim on everyone and everything, how is his authority exercised? What kind of power are we talking about?

When things break down we look for answers, for a source of truth and authority. In the encyclical *Fides et Ratio (Faith and Reason)* that came out in 1998, the Pope spoke to the issue of ultimate truths in the midst of ethical confusion and despair. His letter rightly stood against a merely utilitarian view of life: there *are* things we can believe and hold on to. We need to recapture the liberating power of the sacredness of human life and the spiritual energy that is available to us when we accept our God-given dignity and understand that God has given us the ability to know and to do the truth.

The Pope is right: we need the courage to ask big questions again. Don't be afraid to think: what are you *for*? what are you *about*? To whom or to what have you given your allegiance? Who or what rules your life? The church at its best is no stranger to this journey of discovery. We believe that we have received the gift of ultimate truth about human life in the Easter mystery of death and resurrection. We believe that the deepest truth of our lives has to do with dying and being raised to new life.

But how are these claims pressed truthfully? These are big claims and easily misunderstood. That is why the Pope was also right to apologize to the world for the sins of Christians through the ages. Christians have often pressed their claim to truth untruthfully. The maxim that justified religious repression was "Error has no rights!" This may be objectively true, but only God is the final judge. When the church—with all its failings—saw itself as the sole arbiter of truth, many people were severely damaged by its adamant and sometimes cruel authority.

At their best, Christians make some amazing and generous assumptions about human beings. Perhaps the most daring of all is the concept of the person as a free and intelligent subject with the capacity to know God, truth and goodness. The reign of God is about freedom.

So, what are the *absolutes* of Christ as the truth? Ted King, the late Dean of Cape Town, identifies two kinds of people in the New Testament whom Jesus condemned: those who thought themselves superior and those who had no compassion. Those two kinds of people tell us something about the authority of Christ. Look at Christ on the cross. What does it tell you about divine authority? Jesus is not offensive in what he says, but in who he is. He himself is the offense. This broken and ruined person, this man on the cross, is king! "All of you will be offended in me." And who are the offended? This generation—the wise and the intelligent, and the Pharisees. That covers most of us.

Given a king reigning from the cross, how should Christian claims be pressed? By bullying? By torture? By imprisonment? Look at him! If this is the Lord of the Universe, how is the truth to be expressed? The double mystery of our humanity and God's gentle power is celebrated in the eucharist, bread broken and given away. To be fully yourself, you have to find a way of giving yourself away. The truth requires our surrender. We think we are self-possessed, but when we surrender to the truth we are shaken out of our self-possession. Sometimes we suffer oppression by others, but more often we are the perpetrators of our own spiritual imprisonment. We live with two contradictory desires: the longing for self-possession and the desire to be knocked off our perch and pushed into a greater and deeper reality. The mystery of freedom is this:

we find our souls when we surrender to the sovereign power within us who made us and who loves us.

The gospel sees us in a radically different light as people with an inherent dignity, worthy of respect, unique and precious images of God. To be a person is to enjoy an identity secure in God. The good news is that your value doesn't evaporate if you feel meaningless or are in pain. Nor does it end "if you are no longer young or attractive. It doesn't stop when you are drunk, comatose, or imprisoned. It is not based on your actions, productivity, or achievement. It is based on the fact that you are a person." There is, in short, a dignity about existence itself. The psalmist and the saints understood that trees, animals, mountains, and sunsets have value, dignity, and intrinsic goodness, "whether they think so or not, whether we can use them or not."[4]

✆ *The Kingdom of Truth*

To my mind Shakespeare's *King Lear* is his greatest play, reflecting not only Shakespeare's world but much of our own.[5] In *King Lear* there is a crisis of authority, which amounts to a crisis of truth-telling. Lear wants to give up his kingdom and hand it over to his daughters. In so doing, he creates a crisis of authority. Who is in charge when the king abdicates? To whom do we owe allegiance? A crisis of authority is always a crisis of identity.

Authority. Identity. Truth-telling. They are all linked together. Who am I? Where do I fit into the scheme of things? Lear says to his fool, "Dost thou call me fool, boy?" The fool answers, "All thy other titles thou hast given away. That thou was born with." When everything is stripped away, what's left? Lear later cries, "Doth any here know me? Why, this is not Lear. Doth Lear walk thus, speak thus? *Who is it that can tell me who I am?*" Authority becomes a crisis in times of change; the crisis gets more acute as the changes come faster and become more violent. Imagine what it was like in Shakespeare's time, which is somewhat like ours. On the one hand there was a society that had not yet outgrown its past. Old values were invoked that assumed cooperative and reasonable human decency. "God to be worshipped; parents to be honored; others to be used by us as ourselves would be by them."

King Lear laid aside his authority—his truth—as a monarch and as a father. A terrible tragedy followed: everything that told him who he was was taken away. His crown, his titles, his social position, even his name. When authority goes, the questions multiply. Who am I and where do I belong? What is the truth that holds my life together? We see power and authority reduced to rags, and this is what is so marvelous about the gospel. Jesus calls us into covenant and conversion, into betrothal and marriage. The world is a wedding, and everyone is invited!

There we recover our own royal nature. It is a glorious thing to be a human being. Our royal nature is rediscovered by a conversion to humility, to tenderness, to love, to patience, to forgiveness. Such things express our royal nature. All in the service of the one "who service is perfect freedom." King Lear asks, "Will someone tell me who I am?" The answer? You are a child of God and a guest and host of the world.

Story and fact are always in uneasy tension with each other, no matter how carefully we line up the historical data, or how honestly we report the events through which we have lived. These do not, themselves, tell the story of our lives. Getting the facts straight is not enough to find the story to which they belong. That is why we tell the stories in the context of worship, day after day and week after week. That is why we break the bread. This amazing bread-breaking is the story into which the facts of our life, no matter how despicable or sad or regretted, are put in the context of hope. Covenants come about when we share stories. When we share stories, it becomes hard for us to use "truth" as a weapon to hurt others.

We have been promised a kingdom of truth that cannot be shaken. The ruler of this kingdom is Jesus Christ, who is the truth. But what are we to make of these strange claims? As we have seen, truth—in these instances—cannot be propositional "truths." Truth, in the sense of a kingdom and person, must be of a different order than fact. The truth of divine power, while deeply disturbing to us, speaks to us of love.

Meanwhile, back on planet earth, things look very different. When I returned from summer vacation a few years ago I discovered that one of the stained-glass windows of the Chapel of Grace at the cathedral where I work had been vandalized. Someone had hurled a brick through the crucifixion. That is routine in churches nowadays, but what, I wondered, is the *truth* of it? Who threw the rock? A madman? A distressed and disgruntled homeless person with no bed for the night? When we try to discover the whole truth about an event, there is an ever-widening circle of stories to be told. That same summer people had been slaughtered in Ireland (on the Feast of the Assumption, the Feast of Our Lady). Terrorism broke out in East Africa and the United States made a bloody response in Afghanistan and the Sudan. These seemed hardly signs of the kingdom of God, God's truth.

The scriptures call this condition "a covenant with death," which is another way of saying that we have joined ourselves to a great lie. The lie is that we think that we can cheat death and live under our own power. The prophet Isaiah rebukes the "scoffers" who rule Jerusalem and say, "We have made a covenant with death...; when the overwhelming scourge passes through it will not come to us; for we have made lies our refuge, and in falsehood we have taken shelter" (Isaiah 28:14-15). But those who follow Christ are given the kingdom that cannot be shaken:

God's foundation stone, God's true north, is Jesus. When we look around and see the crisis in the world, we ask ourselves, how is the kingdom to be restored? How is the covenant made good?

The covenant is restored when we understand that truth-telling and storytelling bind us together. What you think is the truth depends on what you believe. What we believe about what it is to be human affects the way we arrange the facts of life and turn them into a story. In the church and in the synagogue we tell stories. The story of the Fall at the beginning of Genesis comes to mind. If you are a Christian who is even half-awake, you don't go around saying, "Ugh! Human beings are sinners—what a surprise! I never knew that!" The story of redemption tells us that our choices matter, the conviction that the last word about us is a tough word of love.

We believe that drama, and the drama of the eucharist in particular, can change people's lives for the better. We share in a meal that seals our covenant with God and with each other. It is binding. It is a betrothal. The truth of God's kingdom is, *there is but one human heart.* Oh yes, we are committed to truth-telling, but truth-telling means locating the story in which all the facts fit. Judas betrayed Christ—that is a fact. But into which story does it truly fit?

    ∾ *Facts only make sense in the context of a story. We only make sense in the context of a covenant.*

You are the temple of the Holy Spirit. This does not mean that there are not painful decisions to be made. Something terrible happens to us when we lose aspects of our freedom. When I am dying (in whatever state I am in) I hope that I will be part of a community of trust and love that understands the *intrinsic* value of human life. As long as I am a member of Christ, my living and dying as a person who is known, loved, and accepted is what really matters. From the perspective of the gospel we are liberated to believe in ourselves because God believes in us, even at our worst. How we act depends to a large extent on who we believe ourselves to be. And who we really are is safe in the hands of God, whose love sometimes burns us before it transforms us. And this is the truth.

Endnotes

◈ 1. The Truth About John

1. Neil Postman, *Technopoly* (New York: Knopf, 1992), 69-70.
2. Arthur Miller, *Timebends* (New York: Harper, 1987), 482.
3. Bruce Robinson, *The Peculiar Memories of Thomas Penman* (Woodstock, N. Y.: Overlook Press, 1998), 199.
4. Quoted by Sallie McFague, "Should a Christian Love Nature?" in *Earth Letter* (September 1993). See also Iris Murdoch's *The Sovereignty of Good* (London: Routledge & K. Paul, 1970) and "The Sublime and the Good" in *Chicago Review* 13 (1959): 51.

◈ 2. Respect for the Facts

1. Donald McCullough, *Say Please, Say Thank You* (New York: Putnam, 1998), 5.
2. See Jonathan Rauch, *Kindly Inquisitors* (Chicago: University of Chicago Press, 1993), 4. The incident took place at Southern Methodist University in 1990.
3. See Susan Haack's "Staying for an Answer: The Untidy Process of Groping for Truth" in *The Times Literary Supplement* (July 9, 1999), 12. Note also her book, *Manifesto of a Passionate Moderate* (Chicago: University of Chicago Press, 1998).
4. Raymond Tallis, "Will the Real Stanley Fish Stand Up, Please?" *The Times Literary Supplement* (February 25, 2000), 6.

5. Jacob Needleman, *Time and the Soul* (New York: Doubleday, 1998), 13-14.

6. Ibid., 75.

7. Ken Wilbur, *A Brief History of Everything* (Boston: Shambala, 1996), 107-108.

8. Ibid., 91.

๛ *3. Finding a Story Faithful to the Facts*

1. E. H. Carr, *What is History?* (New York: Vintage Books, 1961).

2. Mary Gordon, *The Other Side* (New York: Penguin, 1990), 33, 57.

3. See Gil Bailie, *Violence Unveiled* (New York: Crossroad, 1995), 365.

4. Diogenes Allen, *Temptation* (Cambridge, Mass.: Cowley, 1986), 62-63.

5. A. N. Wilson, *God's Funeral* (New York: Norton, 1999), 13.

6. Needleman, *Time and the Soul*, 62-63.

7. Victoria Clark, "The Martyr Complex of the Serbs," *The Tablet* (May 15, 1999), 648.

8. Michael Ignatieff, "The Elusive God of War Trials," *Harpers* (March 1997) 15ff. *Italics mine.*

๛ *4. The Craft of Truth-Telling*

1. The writings of Peter Brook about the theater have been helpful to me over the years, especially *The Empty Space* (1968) and *There Are No Secrets* (1993).

2. Peter Brook, *There Are No Secrets* (London: Methuen, 1993), 16-17.

3. Ibid., 21.

4. Ibid., 23.

5. Robertson Davies, *Murther and Walking Spirits* (New York: Viking, 1991), 321-23.

6. William Gass, "The Art of the Self," *Harpers* (May 1994), 50.

∿ 5. Stories That Hold Us Together

1. David Malouf, *Remembering Babylon* (London and New York: Random House, 1994), 59.

2. Dennis E. Kenny, "Clinical Pastoral Education—Exploring Covenants with God" in *The Journal of Pastoral Care* (June 1980) 34:2.

3. See Michael Ignatieff's review of Elaine Showalter's *Hysteries: Hysterical Epidemics and Mass Culture* in *The London Review of Books* (July 17, 1997).

4. Walter Brueggemann, "Preaching a Sub-Version" in *Theology Today* (July 1998), 196. This section owes a great deal to his article.

5. Ibid.

6. Michael Lewis, *The New New Thing* (London: Hodder and Stoughton, 1999), 84.

7. Bernard McGinn, *The Growth of Mysticism: Gregory the Great through the 12th Century* (New York: Crossroad, 1994), 103.

8. Ibid., 58.

9. Ibid., 94.

10. Ibid., 97.

∿ 6. Truth and Cunning

1. Thomas Mann, *The Magic Mountain*, trans. John E. Wood (New York: Knopf, 1995), 271-72.

2. Stephen Carter, "The Etiquette of Democracy" in *Christian Century* (April 8, 1998), 366.

3. Stephen Carter, *Civility: Manners, Morals, and the Etiquette of Democracy* (New York: Basic Books, 1998), 39.

4. Lewis Hyde, *Trickster Makes the World: Myth, Mischief and Art* (New York: Farrar, Straus & Giroux, 1998), 159-160.

5. Ibid., 304.

6. Quoted in Hyde, 226.

7. Umberto Eco, *The Name of the Rose* (New York: Harcourt Brace Jovanovich, 1983), 491.

8. Calvin Tomkins, *Duchamp: A Biography* (New York: Holt, 1996), 449-450.

∾ 7. Pilgrims of the Truth

1. John Bunyan, *Pilgrim's Progress,* ed. Roger Sharrock (London: Penguin, 1965), 372. All further references are to this edition.

2. John Updike, *Rabbit Run* (New York: Knopf, 1960), 127.

3. Quoted in Angela Tilby, *Soul: God, Self, and the New Cosmology* (New York: Doubleday, 1992), 223.

4. Eric James, *A Time to Speak* (London: SPCK, 1997), 163.

5. Quoted in Frederick Buechner, *The Eyes of the Heart* (San Francisco: HarperSanFrancisco, 1999).

6. Terry Waite, *Taken on Trust* (New York: Harcourt Brace Jovanovich, 1993), from the foreword.

7. See David Whyte, *The Heart Aroused* (New York: Doubleday, 1994), 182ff.

∾ 8. Truth as Betrothal

1. Michael Ventura as quoted in *The Sun* (September 1999).

2. Quoted by Cornell West in *Race Matters* (New York: Vintage, 1994), 119.

3. D. Oken, "What to tell cancer patients" in *Journal of the American Medical Association* (1961) 175: 1120-28; D. Novack, *et al,* "Changes in physicians' attitudes toward telling the cancer patient" in *Journal of the American Medical Association* (1979) 241: 897-900.

4. Jean Shinoda Bolen, *Ring of Power* (San Francisco: Harper, 1992), 10.

5. Jean Bethke Elshtain, *Democracy On Trial* (New York: Basic Books, 1995), 40.

6. Donald McCullough, *Say Please, Say Thank You* (New York: G. P. Putnam, 1998).

7. Peter Jay writing in *The Times* (October 7, 1994), 17.

8. Abraham Heschel, *Who is Man?* (Stanford: Stanford University Press, 1965).

9. Quoted by Alan Ecclestone, *Gather the Fragments* (Sheffield, Eng.: Cairns Publications, 1994), 103.

10. Brian K. Smith, "Christianity as a Second Language," *Theology Today* (January 1997), 448.

11. Lionel Blue, *The Tablet* (August 1998), 1083.

∾ 9. Truth as Moral Adventure

1. Anne Sexton, *The Awful Rowing Toward God* (Boston: Houghton Mifflin, 1975), 61.

2. Umberto Eco, *The Name of the Rose* (New York: Harcourt Brace Jovanovich, 1983), 492.

3. See Iris Murdoch, *The Nice and the Good* (New York: Viking, 1968).

∾ 10. Wonder and Gratitude

1. This section and what follows owes a great deal to Nigel Biggar's *Good Life: Reflections on What We Value Today* (London: SPCK, 1997).

2. Martha Nussbaum, *Poetic Justice* (Boston: Beacon, 1995), 38-39.

3. Garry Wills, *Saint Augustine* (New York: Viking, 1999), xii.

4. Cynthia Bourgeault, *Love is Stronger Than Death* (New York: Bell Tower, 1999), 114-115.

∾ 11. The Music of Trust

1. Stephen Carter, *The Culture of Disbelief* (New York: Basic Books, 1993), 71.

2. Gil Bailie, *Violence Unveiled* (New York: Crossroad, 1995), 40.

3. John W. Gardner, *Building Community* (Washington, D.C.: Independent Sector, 1991), 15.

∾ 12. The Kingdom of Love and Truth

1. A. N. Wilson, *Daughters of Albion* (New York: Viking, 1991), 242. *Italics mine.*

2. I am indebted to my friend Robert Kirschner for this story from the Yiddish writer, Isaac Loeb Peretz, a creator of Jewish and Hasidic tales, who died in Warsaw in 1915.

3. Thomas Cahill, *How the Irish Saved Civilization* (New York: Doubleday, 1995), 217-18.

4. John K. Kavanaugh, "Death's Dignity" in *America* (April 1997).

5. I am indebted to Eric James, *A Time to Speak*, 182ff, for this section on *King Lear*.

Cowley Publications is a ministry of the Society of St. John the Evangelist, a religious community for men in the Episcopal Church. Emerging from the Society's tradition of prayer, theological reflection, and diversity of mission, the press is centered in the rich heritage of the Anglican Communion.

Cowley Publications seeks to provide books, audio cassettes, and other resources for the ongoing theological exploration and spiritual development of the Episcopal Church and others in the body of Christ. To this end, it is dedicated to developing a new generation of theological writers, encouraging them to produce timely, creative, and stimulating publications of excellence, and making these publications available widely, reaching both clergy and lay persons.